T0158891

THE EYES
OF OUR CHILDREN

Laura D. Distarce

BALBOA.
PRESS

A DIVISION OF HAY HOUSE

Balboa Press books may be ordered through booksellers or by contacting:

Balboa Press
A Division of Hay House
1663 Liberty Drive
Bloomington, IN 47403
www.balboapress.com
1 (877) 407-4847

Because of the dynamic nature of the Internet, any web addresses or links contained in this book may have changed since publication and may no longer be valid. The views expressed in this work are solely those of the author and do not necessarily reflect the views of the publisher, and the publisher hereby disclaims any responsibility for them.

The author of this book does not dispense medical advice or prescribe the use of any technique as a form of treatment for physical, emotional, or medical problems without the advice of a physician, either directly or indirectly. The intent of the author is only to offer information of a general nature to help you in your quest for emotional and spiritual well-being. In the event you use any of the information in this book for yourself, which is your constitutional right, the author and the publisher assume no responsibility for your actions.

Any people depicted in stock imagery provided by Thinkstock are models, and such images are being used for illustrative purposes only.
Certain stock imagery © Thinkstock.

Print information available on the last page.

ISBN: 978-1-5043-7504-7 (sc)
ISBN: 978-1-5043-7506-1 (hc)
ISBN: 978-1-5043-7505-4 (e)

Library of Congress Control Number: 2017902382

Balboa Press rev. date: 03/24/2017

The Eyes of Our Children

The eyes of our children are upon us
Do not look away
For in their eyes we see ourselves reflected
It is we they save

Let them draw us in for they hold the keys
To the treasures we only dream about
Take them by the hand
And let them lead us
For in their innocence
Are the wonders we desire

Beware no harm comes to them –
They walk with angels
And shine their brilliance
And touch us with their gentleness

Oh take delight in them
They are free
They break our chains that bind us to the past
And show the promise of a new day
The eyes of our children are upon us
Do not look away

Laura Distarce

INTRODUCTION

Someone needs to say this.
Who am I you might ask. What qualifies me to write this.
There are no letters after my name to indicate years spent in schooling.
But schooling I have had.
I don't hold an important place in business.
But I do have work.

I am a woman, a mother.
I have a voice.

It seems to me that there is an awful lot of time and energy spent
proving our rights - God-given rights upon which this country was founded -
Life, Liberty and the Pursuit of Happiness.

Not rights meant only for some.
Not rights meant for whoever is stronger,
bigger, richer, or was here first.

*"…One Nation (under God), Indivisible, with Liberty and Justice for **All***"
We pledge allegiance for this protection.
We recite the words but don't pay much attention to their content.
Who recites the Pledge of Allegiance?
Our very own Mission Statement.
Our children recite it.

Yes, some things need to be said.
Why me?
Why not?

DEDICATION

This is dedicated to my children,
Joseph and Edward,
the wise men I share Life with;

to children everywhere
for they are the best work that we do;

and to the child within every adult
who longs to be healed and free.

And because children are so "recently from God
they still remember" I will heed the wise words of my sons:

"Keep it simple."

PREFACE

I think it important to explain the writings in this book. All the writings are original unless noted.

In 1994 I took a class in **The Artist's Way** by Julia Cameron. It is a book about "unblocking creativity" and Julia had been teaching this process for many years before putting it in book form so that many more could benefit from her wisdom and experience.

As part of the process one must commit to writing "Morning Pages" – 3 pages, handwritten, first thing in the morning. I committed to Morning Pages and have been writing them ever since – more than 24 years now. I like to call myself a student and facilitator of The Artist's Way. Over the years, I have revisited the book and have facilitated its process for myself and others. Each time has brought new insights and clarity.

Early in the process I had voiced a desire to be a writer, and eventually many of the pieces in this book came through my Pages. At the same time I was raising my two sons whose presence in my life profoundly changed me and my beliefs.

In the process of unblocking creativity, I also came to a greater understanding and connection with my Source, which I call God. I also have a greater understanding, appreciation and gratitude for the unique contribution I make to the healing of the World – and that all can make – most especially our children.

GOD'S CHILD

There is a Child in each of us who longs to be honored and seen,
who wishes to be safe and free.

THIS IS GOD'S CHILD!

This is the Child who was last, and now shall be first.
This is the Child who shall lead.
This Child of God is loved and loving.
This Child of God knows who it is.
This Child of God is Joy and Peace,
Understanding and Compassion.
This Child of God sings and dances,
and delights in its own Being.
This Child of God believes in wonder and magic, and that
Anything is possible!
This Child of God is full of light and grace.
This is the Godstuff already within us that is waiting to express –
when we feel safe.
This day, we pray......
We know we are safe, wherever we are,
for God is always with us,
and shows us our way.
YES!
With the love and support of the Universe,
With God as our foundation stone,
We can do all things!

We can create a world that is safe for ALL God's Children.
And so it is. And so it shall be.

1

FINDING MY VOICE

I didn't always feel I had a voice. Contrary to how things appeared I felt quite invisible for a major portion of my life. But I see now it was how things were supposed to be. For when you are 'invisible' you can be quite observant - of people, of life, of the way things happen.

I am in no way a victim. I had issues. I had lessons. But I've dealt with them, am dealing with them. It's a continual process. It's called LIFE. It doesn't end just because we have reached adulthood. I learned the valuable insights those issues and lessons brought me, and continue to bring me. I learned that I could change. I learned that Life **is** about change.

I have a voice, just like everyone else. Now that is a revelation! I have often gone into a library or a book store and just looked at all the books - wow! Every one of those books represents someone's voice - someone's experience or someone's fantasy. Someone's idea that came to fruition. It is awesome and intimidating at the same time. Other people surely had important things to say. But me?
I can let you be the judge of how important they are, I just feel they need to be said. Not that these things haven't been said before. I bring no new formulas, just perhaps a different way to see things, a different way to connect the experiences of our lives. Another voice having courage to speak about issues that have heart and meaning for me.

All human beings are expressive beings, because essentially we are creative beings. My expression is words, something that surprises and delights me. I love to write; remember when I decided that I would write as a means to express my emerging voice.

All human beings wish to be seen and heard; honored for our right to be. While on paper we cherish those words in practice those rights must be **proven**. Back when our country was founded, those "rights" were intended for just some. As our country was being explored and settled, we understood those rights to mean 'some deserve to be here more than others'. More than indigenous people living here for thousands of years before we ever set foot on this continent.

I grew up in this country, in New Jersey, of Italian/Irish/German heritage. I went through parochial elementary school, public high school, and two years of college in New York City before moving to California where I eventually obtained a B.A. degree. More than anything else I learned was this: "History is written by those in power."

What occurs to me is that over the past twenty-five years or more, History has been re-written, and that has unsettled us more than we care to admit. Truth always comes out, and what has come out has slowly and painfully made us more aware, has eroded our confidence and trust in the people we were told we could trust, and has set us adrift from our moorings. In short, we have lost our direction. We can't find our heart, or rather, it's buried under the pain of our grief. We certainly don't remember joy; was it possible we ever felt it? And after years of constant bombardment by advertisers we're not even sure just whose life we're living. We're in a mess!

Each time we are made aware of the corruption, the injustice, the senseless acts of people we previously trusted, we come undone. But things must come apart before they can heal and come back together whole. There is always great chaos before there is great harmony, so I am hopeful.

We are sadly out of balance. We need to call a halt to the way we are living. We need to stop consuming more than we need and hoarding more than we use. It is wisdom that says "our strength becomes what we focus our attention on". We need to refocus.

***

When people are not honored for who they are and their right to be, they battle. It's the survivor mode. They not only have to prove their rights, they also have to get in someone's face to be heard. Honestly, as a woman in this society, I've had to battle. Our Society doesn't value women. Many societies around the world do not honor women; do not see them as equal to men – equal in value. Why do we have to prove that? Why do we have to get in someone's face to be heard? And then get blasted for unlady-like behavior? Even our behavior has become dysfunctional, and we don't even know it. We laugh when we ought to be crying. We are numb; we can't even feel anymore.

I've been angry. And I'm a white woman! My rage has not caused me to kill anyone, but I thought about it. Instead, we turn the rage back on ourselves, proving we are worthy in over-extension patterns that declare we can do it. Do what?

I always wondered who had this right to decide how my life should be? Then I learned I had "choices". Women have choices? Yeah, women have choices. All human beings have choices.

My mother never told me or taught me that I had value. She assumed that Society would take care of me because I was white. We white women come to the game late. It's not a 'white' society. It's a 'white **man's** society'. And no woman is valued. I can already hear disagreement. But even if you're a woman reading this who was valued, there are too many more who weren't, and aren't. And if you are a man, especially a white man reading this, I hope you do or have done some profound soul-searching.

We can end the debate over which race is superior. Science tells us that there are no differences between the races genetically. The only differences lie in "opportunity". Opportunity to experience life, liberty, justice, and happiness.

I haven't much liked the patterns that emerged as I worked to prove my worth. Patterns that have led to aggressiveness, gross over-extension, weariness, burn-out, echoing words every good American must have had drummed into them since birth: "You want to get ahead? Work harder!"

Yes, there's been a double standard of conduct between men and women. It pervades all aspects of our lives. If we knew it in our personal lives, it makes sense that it would spill over into the business world.

Women have had to fight for economic equality. It is fair that women and men be paid equally for the same work. The Women's Movement was fair and just. Women thought their voices would be counted when they were on an equal par with men economically. Essentially, they followed the rules: Money talks, so fight for equal pay and you'll have a voice. You know, I don't much like the rules; who made them anyway? They aren't fair, in fact they're 'stacked' against most of us ever getting ahead. It will take a long time this way before the barriers break down to allow women their voices and their places in the world.

"Work a little harder, Honey." I'm not adverse to hard work. I am adverse to a treadmill of constant doing, constant proving. It attacks my worth, tries to convince me I am not enough.

Nope, I don't like the rules, don't much like the game. It doesn't work for everyone, so ultimately it works for no one. Could we just stop a minute and think about what we are doing – to ourselves, to each other, to our earth?

* * *

I suppose the only thing that has sustained me over the years is that I have always believed in love; that love is most important; that we have a great capacity to love, we just don't know how. How do we understand something very few of us have had first- hand experience with – true love. We all wish it (be honest). **True love is unconditional love**, and very few of us ever experienced that! We do keep trying. Well I kept trying.

In my thirties, I had two children. Boys. I thought God must have given me boys so that I could raise them to be a different kind of man. Somehow, intuitively I knew I must raise them to be 'partners'.

I had progressed far enough in my own issues to realize that I made a far better parent in my thirties. I had more confidence, more awareness. I was reasonably happy. But I had ventured into parenting only slightly prepared. Aside from a couple of courses in college having to do with child development, the only education I had was the one I picked up through my own parents.

Right here, I'll have to say that I do love my parents; that I am grateful for all they did for me. I acknowledge that they did the best they could; they too were products of their own experiences and the mindset of the times in which they lived. I understand all that. In my understanding, I also am aware that they passed on some very dysfunctional patterns. And I can forgive them their shortcomings. I can see all of them, and that's why I can love them and let go of what no longer works.

I'm not sure it's just been my experience, or if this is the Time when we finally "get it" and do an about-face. *My children changed my life.*

They turned me around, and showed me what was important, and what I had forgotten, and I truly hope that I shall never be the same! I thought I would teach them and truthfully, I have, but they have taught me more! Are we not all teachers and students? Yes, we are.

***

We live in a violent society. 'Shoot 'um up', just like in the movies. Declare war, hey, it's good for the economy, right? We've lost our ability to talk to each other when we disagree. In truth, I don't believe we ever really knew how to communicate, not when the 'rules' say you have to get angry before someone will listen.

Anger unchecked becomes violence. And violence, at its deepest level, is a cry from the soul. Why are our children becoming violent? They are desperately trying to get our attention, and they are resorting to what they have seen adults use and works.

I'd like to put forth some things to look at in a different way and things to ponder and talk about, in a dialogue not a debate. What we are willing to look at can change.
And no matter what anyone says, the world can change - one person at a time if need be. I've been called a "bliss bunny", and lots of other things for having too optimistic an attitude. Told to "get real". Told I'm not practical. A Pollyanna. If you remember, Pollyanna turned around a whole town!

I've been told I have no 'common sense'. And those people were right.........I have 'uncommon sense'.

Here's the deal: I don't much care what you call me. My self-worth is intact, and whatever you think you can dig up on me to discredit me probably won't stop me. I'd rather try other ways than continue the way we are going.

I'm quite visual and in my mind's eye I seen "patterns". It looks like we are truly headed off the edge of the world! We keep consuming and prizing our technology over preserving and thinking with our hearts. Thank God the world is round! (as opposed to flat) Which means that 1. We won't fall off. 2. We come back around to where we started. Will we be wiser and make different choices, or continue virtual "Groundhog's Day"? 3. As we march our own selves to victory, we must also turn around to help those behind us. It's the looping back that closes the circle and guarantees we won't fall off the edge, and insures that we all move forward together. If you can visualize this, you will have understood a very important pattern.

We are out of balance, way out of balance. It's no longer acceptable, as a people who prize our minds, to discard Truth because it does not fit our Western ideologies. It is from Eastern ideologies that we learn every living organism is made up of masculine and feminine energy, the yin and yang. Our children know this – ask them! Our masculine energy has dominated, and we must acknowledge the feminine energy, honor it and let it bring us back into balance….in ourselves, our society, our world.

What do we honor that is feminine? We have gotten so polarized, especially in this country, that we believe men are masculine and women are feminine, and we don't understand that we human beings have both energies. What we don't understand is that all thought (ideas, inspiration) creativity itself, originates from the feminine.

But "men are from Mars, and women are from Venus"! Some men, and some women. But I do believe that men can have hearts, and woman can be strong and have a voice.

We call the earth **Mother** Earth, yet we defile her. Who decided it was O.K. to concrete over every inch of land, cutting down trees, destroying natural habitats, not only for animals but also for the natives already living on the continent? Where is it written that anyone has that right?

We do not honor Mother anything! Beginning with the earth. Remember the T.V. commercial about the butter – "It's not nice to fool Mother Nature"? No, it's not nice and she can't be fooled. The joke is on us! We will lose unless we change the way we live.

TRUTH IS UNCOMFORTABLE

Something happens when you discover you have a voice. It's like the dam breaks and you can't hold back any longer. People say you talk too much, but I question that. Yes, you might become slightly unbalanced in the other direction, but that's only for a time, and so, with practice, you adjust. I don't think it's really that you talk too much, it's what you are saying that disturbs people, especially if what you are saying is Truth.

I've been advised to 'say things in a non-combative way', I've been advised to keep silent by other women who haven't yet found their own voices. I've been told "don't rock the boat"! Though I truly strive to communicate for understanding and don't wish to offend, you just can't tell the Truth and not make people uncomfortable! And that *is* the truth!

What is my intention? To find Truth. And when Truth presents Itself, you move toward it, like magnets. I have a passion for Truth which translates into a passion for Life - all Life. *All Life is sacred.*

You can decide for yourself. You can say it's just my opinion. But Truth resonates deep in the soul, and it will wrench your gut and stir your insides. I don't make you feel uncomfortable. I'm just the messenger. (History shows we shoot the messenger, which could also cause **me** to feel uncomfortable.) Truth makes you feel uncomfortable. Why? Because it challenges every belief you hold about yourself, your world, and what you are doing in it. It challenges the status-quo.

I often think about Rev. Martin Luther King and the monumental task put before him. His conviction that equality was meant for all people certainly made some people very uncomfortable. He confronted the belief systems that prevailed at the time, and he challenged them in a non-violent way. He understood that equality, liberty, and pursuit of happiness were fundamental rights accorded to all people, not just white people. This was his Work, and he gave his life that all God's children would enjoy these rights.

Martin Luther King was very clear that the Civil Rights Movement was not just for black people. This Movement was for people of all races. No one is free until we all are free. No one. I hear Dr. King's words: "how long?" It's been too long. No one should have to fight. No one should have to be in someone's face to be seen. No one should have to resort to violent means to get attention.
No one.....especially our children.

Here's an uncomfortable Truth: Our children are desperately trying to get our attention. That children resort to violence is our collective shame.

Here's another Truth: Usually we can't relate to things that happen in the world until those things happen to us. We can no longer say that violence would never occur in our communities.

When we are living in safe communities and our lives are going along just swimmingly, we tend to point fingers when violence breaks out in someone else's backyard. Those of us with some awareness and honesty know that we are saying our prayers at night that it hasn't happened to us! Because it could happen anywhere and has in recent times. And the more we think we can build higher walls, or more prisons to keep the violence away from us, the more we come to understand that violence is everyone's issue.

Here's more Truth, and it's very uncomfortable: Who in Congress today can truly say they represent me?....a woman, a mother, working a second job that almost makes ends meet because the first and most important job pays nothing. Didn't the idea of "no taxation without representation" cause a small revolution in our early History? I'm not supporting such violent measures, but the issues are no less important because I'd rather sit down and talk about other solutions.

I am humbled to admit that I wouldn't have found this insight if the issues hadn't landed in my own lap. And for that I ask forgiveness, that I may have at some time in my life not only misunderstood, but did not offer assistance to those who were crying out for help.

Really, who is paying attention?

The gap is widening between those that live a comfortable life and those that don't live even a decent life. We don't and never did begin with a level playing field. We don't play by the same rules, never did.

But even children know – you play fair.

CHILDREN PAY ATTENTION

Children pay very close attention. I don't think they want the world we have created for them. They watch us and they listen. They see and hear far more than we admit. They see adults who have lost their joy for living. They hear adults worry about their jobs, and talk about money as if it were God, which in fact, it has become.

We value what makes money. We put a monetary price on everything to declare its worth.

Children hear that 'those with the money have the power'. They feel they have no voice because they have no value - because they make no money. They get told "wait 'til you grow up" and they reply "what for?"

They try to get our attention.

And yet we are aghast when children, who wish to be seen and heard, will use the same methods that adults use to accomplish this. They get up in our faces, and in extremes, resort to violence. There's a song that says "children have to be carefully taught". We understand, sometimes too late, that hatred is taught. Prejudice is taught. Children learn to solve their problems by watching how adults solve theirs. They learn best by example. They are confused by what they see and hear.
So am I.

Cynicism is created when people say one thing and do another. Words and actions are not aligned. Which do we trust? We wind up trusting neither.

Children have become cynical. And cynical children soon grow to be apathetic adults. And if anything is true, we must acknowledge the apathy that pervades our lives; has crept up on us over time, and has eroded our faith and our trust. Who is telling the truth? For we too were children once. We, too, watched and listened to adults say one thing and do another.

And as adults we are passing that on to our children.

Our children are mirroring us.

Children have an important place in our world.

Children are here to teach us! They are here to make us "turn around".

They not only need our protection and our guidance, they need our attention. They are the Future. They are our most valuable resource. Yes, they need us, *but we need them more.* If we let them do their Work, they will show us our "stuff" - old belief systems that no longer serve us, dysfunctional behavior that is not to be passed on to the next generation. They teach best by example too… their innocence, their joy, their living in the present, their delight in their own being, their constant wonder at new things to discover. Yes, "they come so recently from the God they still remember." And their Work is to remind us, because we have forgotten.

Children show us what matters. Things don't matter. Loving matters. And children are loving. We, in our natural state, are loving.

VALUE

All of us have value – equal value. What that means is that men, women, and children have the same value. No one is more important than anyone else. Neither is one race more important than another race, or one's ethnicity, and certainly not one's gender.

People living in America are not more important than people living in Asia.

Equal *value*.

The Women's Movement steadily made strides to bring women the same value as men enjoyed. Their demands for a voice (vote) and equal pay in the workplace were fair. But I believe they went after the wrong power. While having a share in economic power is slowly making inroads for women, the power they must recognize and claim is authentic power – their right to BE. And when they recognize that and acknowledge that, they no longer put their energy into proving their worth. The women's movement hasn't failed as some would like to believe. It's just gone underground to regroup. What's emerging is a woman who knows her Worth. And that's Power!

What has happened in our Society is that money determines our value, and our voice. I've heard people say "the Golden Rule is those that have the gold, rule". Children don't make money, and don't have a voice (vote). And sadly, our Society doesn't value them.

Money is good! It's a means of exchange. But money is a false security. It can buy us freedom from want, but it cannot buy us freedom from fear. Only LOVE can do that.

I believe there are two things that children must know: 1. that they are loved unconditionally by their parents or care-givers; 2. that they have 'value', that they are valuable - because they all possess a Divine soul.

And they have work as well.

Kahlil Gibran says it best in THE PROPHET:

"Your children are not your children. They are the sons and daughters of Life's longing for itself. They come through you but not from you. And though they are with you yet they belong not to you. You may give them your love but not your thoughts, for they have their own thoughts. You may house their bodies but not their souls, for their souls dwell in the house of tomorrow, which you cannot visit, not even in your dreams. You may strive to be like them, but seek not to make them like you. For life goes not backward nor tarries with yesterday."

FAVORITISM

Many years ago I went into therapy, because, among other things, I could not understand why my siblings did not get along. Yes, our parents had divorced, but I knew many families where parents divorced, and the siblings remained close.

The therapist asked me if there had been 'favoritism' in my family. Yes, I replied, there had, though most likely we'd all disagree about who the favorite was! What he told me next was profound, and stayed with me all these years since. He said that divorce was not what tore our family apart. The family was already fragmented, caused by favoritism. It was favoritism that caused cracks in the foundation. The siblings did not trust each other, and they were each vying for the attention of the parents. A child wanting to get in the parent's good graces would go a long way to 'prove' their worth.

Favoritism is deadly to a family unit. It breeds competition where there should be cooperation.
It fragments and separates. It breeds distrust and overextension to prove our worth. It gives some the idea that they can have power over others because they are the "favored". Slavery is believing one can have power over another.

This idea originated from somewhere. I believe it is the off-shoot of the belief that God has favorites. Yes, some people do believe that God has favorites. For a long time I believed God had favorites, and I wasn't one of them! My own religious upbringing taught me that God demands perfection, and punishes those who do not follow God's rules. It was my religious teachings that made me feel I was unworthy, because the Lord knew, I wasn't perfect. Those teachings

17

did much harm to a young child's mind. The idea that God demands perfection trickles down to how parents discipline their children – for perfection. The notion is completely contrary to the true nature of our Creator – unconditional love, which says "I love you always, and anyway, because you are a child of God."

Out of that root notion that God has favorites comes, in my opinion, an account of fragmentation and separation we call History. Read your History books to know how the idea of favoritism fragmented our human family, separating us from God and each other. Making us have to prove ourselves. Creating distrust, control, and overextension patterns that have become the fabric of our society today.

GOD DOES NOT HAVE FAVORITES.

GOD DEMANDS NOTHING. GOD IS.

We are God's creations. We are God's Family. All of us, as we are, who we are. Who we are and what we think we are, are not quite the same. We have so many labels that define us. But when we peel back the labels to the one we all share – human being, and then build on that, what we truly see is what our Creator truly intended – variety, diversity, uniqueness – but all with a soul, a soul always and forever connected to its Source. A soul that resides within all of God's creation. No need to prove a thing! And if we don't have to prove our existence to God, then why are we killing ourselves (and each other) to prove our existence to anyone else?

I don't believe the crack in the Liberty Bell in Independence Hall in Philadelphia is a fluke. I believe men with good intentions wrote the Declaration of Independence. They were divinely guided to write Truth, but they interpreted its meaning to pertain to only some.

History bears that out. It explains how Thomas Jefferson could write so eloquently about Liberty and yet still own slaves.

I don't know if anyone ever thought about it this way. Favoritism cracked that Liberty Bell. Fragmented us. We may be the richest country in the world, but our foundation is crumbling. A House divided cannot stand (for long)

ON BEING A MOTHER

When I had my children I had the luxury to be home with them for five years. And when I did return to work outside the home I had a job that allowed me to work from home and design my work schedule around my home life. It was truly a gift to do that for I was able to assist in my children's classrooms and their activities all through their grammar school years.

When I had my children there was still the debate over 'working mothers vs. stay-at-home mothers'.

Women wanted voices and economic equality and History has shown that when they went into the work force during World War II, they did not want to give up that power they felt afterwards from earning their own keep. Women like my mother stayed at home and raised children, while their husbands earned a living. Of course, some men did not return from the war and those women were forced into the workplace.

Mothers in the workplace and mothers at home – and while we debated this for many years and its effect on children, I believe there was a bigger issue that no one addressed.

From what I observed, babies don't bond just with mothers – **they bond with the feminine energy in mothers**. And babies can also bond with the feminine energy in fathers. From what I observed, fathers that let that 'softer side' of themselves open to their children create strong bonds from birth.

From what I observed, when fathers honor mothers' work in the home that also creates strong bonds.

When fathers support mothers in their roles, children benefit.

I know of so many mothers who went outside the home to work. Many went because of economic necessity. Many went to find approval – because we all know that our society values what makes money. They didn't find approval in the home. And sadly, when the approval comes from outside the home it will cause a rift in the marriage.

Yes, we need an about-face. Raising children must be our collective work - fathers, mothers, schools, communities – everywhere we live.

We used to enjoy extended families. Many people, many cultures still do. I grew up with lots of siblings, cousins, aunts, uncles, and many traditions that were celebrated.

When I moved to the opposite coast in my twenties, I realized that if I were to thrive, I would have to expand my definition of 'family'.

I recall the lines in Richard Bach's ILLUSIONS:
"your family are those that have joy and respect for your life". I believed that. I trusted those wise words. Forty some years later I can say how true those words are still.

And as I created my own family I could choose what traditions I would continue and even make new ones.

Forty some years later I can affirm the African saying: "It takes a village to raise a child."

***

I have often pondered that if God is everywhere, then God must be in everything. Imagine if we spent time with this idea (instead of proving our worth). Imagine: if God is in every religion then we must study those religions and see what universal truths they offer that we can all adopt. Many scholars have already done this for us. We were given minds for discernment. I have often pondered that cultures and ethnicity must also offer the same.

Traditions that we can all adopt if we wish or traditions we decide no longer serve us because they keep us separated, even from our own true selves.

Honoring diversity is key to our growth as a people, and as a nation, and indeed, the world. The internet has already given us the technology to instantly know what's happening all around the world. Thus far, it has overloaded us with fear and destruction with too little focus on what is beautiful and uplifting. The invention of Facebook has done the same. It connects us too. Again, we have choice. We can use it to further our humanity and to acknowledge we are a 'human family'. There is no stronger bond, and it can break through the fear and doubt that so plagues our world.

It's also interesting to me that since I turned off the evening news over 25 years ago, I no longer live in fear. The world I see and live in is far kinder and generous than what the news media forecasts. Yes, I do "ask" for protection for myself and everyone traveling with me, and because I believe it's possible, that's what happens.

And when I revisit the news it's very obvious that their intention is to keep us in fear, separated, afraid.

I have come to realize: *if it's not good for my children to see, it's not good for me.*

Do yourself a favor: if you haven't already, turn off the news!

***

I believe that even today, we must examine our traditions and beliefs, keep those that work – that work for *everyone* – and discard the old, dysfunctional ones that really never worked except for a few.

"A mother's work is never done." I believe that is true. And neither is a father's. Fortunately, roles are becoming blurred in many places. I don't believe we want to reverse roles either. We just want our world to value, honor and support the sacred work that mothers do. And the sacred beings that women are.

MOTHER ROOT

Creation often needs 2 Hearts
One to root
and One to flower
One to sustain in time of drought
and hold fast against winds of pain
the fragile bloom
That in the glory of its Hour
affirms a heart unsung, unseen

Marilou Awiakta

(embedded in a sidewalk path at University
of California, Riverside)

A MOTHER'S PRAYER

(Ten Commitments of Mothers Everywhere)

To be valued as a woman
To be supported as a mother
To be focused as a parent
To be wise as a counselor
To be conscious as an example
To be cherished as a friend
To be loved as a person
To be forgiven as a human being
To be happy as a child of God
and
To be honored as a bridge
for peace and harmony
all over the world

Laura Distarce
May, 2008

In 1994 for Mother's Day, I wrote this as "A Mother's Wish". Having grown in faith, wisdom and purpose since then, it is now my prayer. I believe it is a timeless prayer, and one that we can all share. Please, pass it on. LD 2013

I LOVE YOU MORE

I became the mother of two boys who were twenty-five months apart in age. Joey was talking in full sentences by the age of one. He wouldn't walk until 17 months and when he did it was on his toes. I was well into my second pregnancy when we took Joey to a pediatric orthopedic doctor, who ruled out cerebral palsy at first because he was so verbal.

He was small for his age and I can remember the surprise on people's faces when I would take him to a restaurant and he could order his own dinner. Many times I was asked if I was a ventriloquist!

I could actually watch his mind work. He would "retrieve" any information he wanted, and I would come to learn that computers were designed to do exactly what our minds do. If it's true that Aquarians are "born 45 years old" then Joey surely fit the bill.

He was to be the master mind for his brother, Eddie, who was the willing accomplice. He couldn't wait for Ed to walk and talk and together, they would be a "team". They each came bearing gifts for my growth and enlightenment.

Joey was breech and so I elected to have a cesarean birth. I never experienced labor. But with Eddie, almost a month before his due date I was experiencing great tightness around my abdomen and after spending an evening at the hospital I was sent home. But a mother knows!

The next day I washed all the baby clothes and got the nursery ready. The day after that I told my husband we needed to go back to the hospital. Within 10 minutes of arriving there, I was on a gurney and

heading for the operating room to have another c-section – this time the baby was in distress!
Even the attending doctor remarked that I had "good instincts".

We all have intuition. As a child I 'knew' things, but my mother discounted them as fantasy and even remarked that I had "too vivid an imagination".

A *mother's* intuition is heightened. She 'knows' things, especially regarding her children and their safety. I would be 'awakened' the moment my children's feet touched the floor.
I trusted that intuition in regard to my children and in raising them. They weren't the same, yet they complimented each other so perfectly.

I think back to my own childhood. I was the middle child of five. I have two older brothers and two younger sisters. We all lived in a small home, all sharing one full bathroom and I shared a bedroom with my sisters. We weren't poor but neither were we rich. Most of the families we knew had lots of kids. We were told that was because we were Catholic. I never had "the talk" with my mother and sex education was definitely *not* taught at our Catholic grammar school, so I didn't understand just where babies came from. "They came from God" I was told.

I wouldn't think much about my life until I visited my Aunt's home on Christmas Eve for a traditional Italian meal. They lived in a big house and had two children who each had their own bedrooms. My young mind made a 'mental note' of this: two's good I thought! (Ironically, today that cousin has five children and I have two!)

As children, we are always assimilating our world into our lives. We are listening and watching and making mental notes: this I will have/be/do when I grow up!

One thing I didn't hear growing up was my parents saying "I love you". I wasn't to hear my father say 'I love you' to me until I was almost 40 years old!

I knew I would always say it to my children, and because of them I said it to my parents.

***

My husband worked a swing shift so he wasn't home for dinner or bedtime. We had a ritual at night.

The boys had baths and then we read a story. Sometimes we watched a movie – the Muppets were always our favorite, especially at Christmas time. When they were small I could sit them beside me in the recliner, and while they watched the show, I could take a 10 minute nap that would revive me. At 8 o'clock they went to bed. I would sit with them on their beds. My Asian neighbors taught me how to massage their feet to relax them, and this works when they are cranky as well. (*and* it works for adults too!)

We would recite a prayer I learned: "My heart shines with love as bright as the sun and the moon and all the stars put together. I wake up happy and have a great day." Then I would tuck them in, kiss them and say 'I love you' to each of them. I still remember the night I did this and as I was leaving the room, Eddie whispered "I love you more."

I can still remember how that felt! And even now the thought of it expands my heart and fills me with thanks that I am a mother and was given the gift of children.

I remember Eddie asking me if all mothers tucked their children into bed at night. "I hope so" I said.

"Why do you ask?" "Well" he said "I go to school with kids who have lots of children in their families. Their mothers must have to start right after dinner!"

Mothers, fathers….whoever is available….
No matter how much technology advances us, we will always need human touch and interaction, no matter how old we are.

LOVING CHILD OF MINE

Loving child of mine
Rest your head on me.
I'll give you shelter
I'll hold you in my arms.
I'll soothe your brow and dry your tears.
I'll lift your pain. Know I am here.
Sweet child of mine
I'll sing you a love song
and rock you gently all night long –
Until you sleep and dream of wonders that can be.
Joyful child of mine, you belong to me.
I'll not ever leave you. No, I never could.
You are the air I breathe –
Loving child in me.
LD

My Experience

Emily Kingsley wrote an essay called "Welcome to Holland" in which she likens having a child with special needs to preparing for a long awaited trip to Italy. One plans their itinerary, practices the language, sets their sights and finally the day comes for the trip. You board the plane and when it lands the stewardess announces "welcome to Holland".
This was not the trip you signed up for!!
Following are my observations from my own experience.

The warning came: *"we will be landing shortly - hold onto your hats, your hearts, and everything you previously knew as familiar landscape"*

And then we landed..... I don't think I'll ever forget how the doctor broke it to me. He advised me to take my son to Danbury School, a designated 'special needs' school in Claremont for a full evaluation of the extent of Joey's *cerebral palsy*. **WHAT???** I said as my heart hit the floor.

I found myself in 'Holland' when my first child, a boy named Joey, was diagnosed with spastic displesia, or mild cerebral palsy at the age of 3.
Preparation for the 'trip' actually began when he was 18 months old, and though he spoke his first word at the age of 6 months, and talked in full sentences by the time he was a year old, he didn't walk until he was 17 months old, and when he did it was on his toes. By the age of 21 months his right leg was turning inward and I knew something was amiss.

Ruling out a variety of things, the doctor recommended that he have physical therapy to stretch hamstrings along with casting and braces. A year later left us all unhappy with the results and so we consented to surgery. It was while in surgery that the doctor confirmed that Joey had spasticity in his ankles.

And so began this experience into parenting a child with special needs.

Joey has a brother, Eddie, who is 2 years younger and considered normal by most standards. And he too, in his own way would challenge the beliefs I held. Both of them have been gifts, and today, as they experience life from the perspective of young adults, I wonder if they truly know how the presence of their lives has impacted mine.

I'd like to share five of the most important things I learned from 'landing in Holland'..........

1. Life happens the way it's supposed to.

This means that we trust life.....we are exactly where we are supposed to be, and we can spend our time and energy resisting that, or, we can trust that there's something very important in this experience and flow with it. As we move into it, we realize that it's not what happens to us in life, but how we respond to what happens to us.

Right from the get-go it seemed people stepped out to guide me. When I took Joey for evaluations at Danbury School, the pre-school teacher there approached me and said Joey would do well in attending their pre-school program. The testing found that Joey was affected in his legs, his gait, and his right side. Mentally he was actually in the 'gifted' range and could and would attend regular school. But for two years Joey went to Danbury, and as is my way, I got involved and was open to all that I would need to learn to help this child of mine. I soon learned that my attitude about my child was going to affect his attitude about himself, and I needed to be clear about that with myself, my child, and anyone else who would impact his life.

2. Your strength becomes what you focus your attention on.

I remember telling Joey about his condition and saying that we could focus on this thing that seemed 'not right', or we could focus on all the other things about him. Joey had already made up his mind. This would not stop him. And it didn't. I volunteered my time at Danbury, and a very wise principal didn't put me in Joey's classroom, but in another class of older children ready to be mainstreamed. As you might know, parents can be overly protective of children, most especially children with special needs.

It was a time of growing for me, a time to learn all I could. I joined the PFA there, and found that many parents felt like I did - intimidated! For many of us, this was our first child, our first experience in school settings, let alone a special needs school setting. For some of us it was the first time we didn't have the ball in our court. We felt helpless, we felt vulnerable, not just for our child, but for ourselves. We realized we were not in control.

When Joey graduated from Danbury, two years later, I was asked to speak as the PFA president to the parents and families of Danbury. I remember telling them that Joey wasn't the only one who graduated. I felt I had graduated too. The experience at Danbury gave me strength, courage and perseverance I didn't know I possessed. I am forever indebted to the staff at Danbury for teaching me to see my child in a different way - to realize there was a gift in this child, and it would be my honor and privilege and part of my own journey to find it.

Which brings me to **3. Children are here to teach us, not the other way around.**

I can say this with unwavering certainty. My child's needs were not extraordinary in relative terms. There were always things I could be grateful for, and I was. I have been asked many times what is it like to have a child with special needs. And my response today is that **all children have special needs**, simply because all human beings are not the same - each is a unique expression. Each comes bearing gifts, each will have needs, just in varying degrees.
All children need our collective attention and focus.

A young friend of mine once asked me if I thought people were capable of loving children that weren't biologically theirs. Before 'landing in Holland' I would have said "No", but fortunately he met me when Joey was well into middle school. I did however, reply that I believed, no matter how they come to us, children should come with a warning label: **"Parents, beware! Your children are here to teach you, not the other way around. It may not be easy, however, it will be enlightening. Are you ready to be enlightened?"**

I found it wasn't children that averted their eyes when seeing my child. I found that they actually were just curious, and if they had insightful parents, they would ask me why Joey wore braces.
And I found myself welcoming those questions, learning to be defenseless and open, because here was an opportunity to educate for understanding and acceptance.

Children perceive differences. They just don't judge them. They accept each other, and truly, we, as adults have forgotten some very fundamental truths in our quest to be grown-up. Yes, you learn a new language in 'Holland'. But you also broaden your previous definition of words like patience, courage, tenacity, success; and you deepen your previous definition of words like compassion, understanding, acceptance, and most importantly - unconditional love.

4. The limiting power of labels

Joey entered the local public school for kindergarten. He wore braces and he carried the label "cerebral palsy" on his transcript. He was the only child in his school with a visible handicap, and that presented challenges on a daily basis. When he was younger, and children asked him why he wore braces, he simply replied "they help me walk". But now, even teachers were questioning his abilities. They assumed that he was mentally challenged, and never asked me the extent of his involvement. Truthfully, here I was again - intimidated with the 'first time' setting of public school, and I didn't know the routine. I DID know my child was gifted and it wasn't until Joey was in 3rd grade that the teachers knew it too. Joey was one of 8 children in the whole school district to be chosen for the gifted program!

I've never much liked labels, and while I know they are important to identify special needs, and the abundance of support that can come from that identification, they pose a challenge to us as well - how to help, but not hinder or limit. The principal at Danbury School warned me that I would have to fight for my child, for he had a label that conjured up all kinds of things in people's minds.

Labeling my son lead me to think about the labels I used to define myself, and others, and over time, to do the demanding work of peeling back those layers of labels that defined me - until I arrived at one we all share - human beings. And that's what I see first, and that's what I build on, and what I build makes me unique, not better or worse - not defensive - just **different**.

What I found was that in some places, it's not OK to be different. And of course, it's not just where I am. It might be any place that doesn't honor diversity or different ways of being. They are 'exclusive' places, rather than 'inclusive'.

Yes, step carefully. Don't get caught up in the limiting power of labels. And don't let others get caught up in them either.

And lastly, and maybe most importantly:

5. *"God doesn't make mistakes"*

If you have just arrived in 'Holland', you may not believe this. You will think it's a detour, but I will tell you, it is not. It may be the road less traveled, but it's the road you're on, and your children have the road map and the directions, and if you pay very close attention, give them acceptance and safety, and all your love and support, they will each bloom the gift that was intended for them **and** you. And sometime, in the hopefully not too distant future, you will realize that you didn't choose 'Holland' - **Holland chose you** - and you will come to know how profoundly this child has changed you, and how sacred and valuable **all** life is, in all its forms.

And you will realize, as I have, that we are not meant to be perfect, we are meant to be loving, and when we are loving, everything **is** perfect.

Spending time in 'Holland' ripped open my heart and showed me how deeply I can love, and how deeply valuable both my children have been to my life experience. It is my experience that there is a God of Infinite Love that works in mysterious ways. I have come to know that Love and trust those ways.

"Life **does** happen the way it's supposed to."

Have faith and trust; know that the right doors will be opened if you knock, if you ask.

Today, I can tell you that the challenges of being a parent are enormous. Very few of us come fully prepared. Stay open, keep learning and growing. Expand your minds, but more importantly - expand your hearts. There's more room in them than you think. This process is the unwinding road we call Life. Slow down! You don't want to miss the details. Stick together! Share what you have and what you learn. The world needs you and your gifts. Not everyone gets to visit 'Holland'.

East Meets West

I write this only in the hope that other women who are mothers and have experienced this know they are not alone and there is help.

I suffered from PMS for a good part of my life. My menstrual cycles were always severe. I remember staying home from school because of the pain. It wasn't until I was married and on birth control that I experienced some relief. Fortunately, when I moved to California I found a doctor who believed my symptoms were real and we tried various remedies; all to no avail.

Then I had two children and the PMS was relentless.
I had what they call "the baby blues" – one minute I'm fine, the next I'm sobbing uncontrollably.
I felt like I had one good week a month. The other three weeks it felt like something invaded my body and took over, and it was affecting my children and my marriage, let alone myself.

One night I was watching the evening news. A young mother had drowned her children. She reportedly had suffered from depression. Just the day before I had spanked my son; only I didn't stop at a swat or two. I knew I was in trouble and I needed to find some help. That news report was my wake-up call.

Some of my friends knew of my PMS troubles. One of them called me to say she had just visited an acupuncturist in town and his brochure said that he could treat PMS. I called and made an appointment.

I remember meeting Matthew and his asking me about my PMS symptoms. He listened to my pulse and looked at my tongue and proceeded to tell me my whole medical history. I was impressed. Then he said with great humbleness "I think I can help you." Thirty minutes later I walked out of his office feeling "even".....something I hadn't felt in years.

I wholeheartedly believe that Matthew saved my life. PMS is a hormone imbalance. I had it before my pregnancies and after my pregnancies the imbalance was even greater. I worked with Matthew for over a year.

Acupuncture is not a 'quick fix'. It is a holistic approach to health and in the process, my other conditions healed as well. I learned how the body can heal itself when the meridians are clear and the energy can flow. That's saying it simplistically. What I also learned is that Eastern medicine is in the business of being well, and Western medicine is in the business of being sick. Western medicine treats the symptoms; Eastern medicine treats the cause.

It's been over 25 years since I first went to Matthew for treatment. He is a gifted healer. I remarked to him that I would sail through menopause because I had treated the hormone imbalances in my body – and I did – no hot flashes, nothing even closely resembling the horrors of menopause.

Though in 25 years acupuncture is coming more into the mainstream as treatment, we need our health care system to allow for this alternative.

I have not been ill in over 10 years. I will get the occasional cold, but not severely. I tell my regular physician: I don't need flu shots and I don't do drugs – especially prescription drugs!

***

Joey was approaching second grade and the doctor was contemplating more surgery. He sent us to a wonderful physical therapist.

Joe already had one surgery to lengthen his hamstrings. It was during this surgery that the doctor realized that Joe has spasticity in his feet and his particular CP is called spastic dysplasia and it affects his gait.

I was seeing Matthew and I asked him to look at Joe. Matthew told me that Joe's whole right side was blocked and that nothing would show improvement because of that.

He even came to a physical therapy appointment with us, and I soon learned that East was meeting West in the medical field. Matthew worked on Joey but at that time he did not believe in using needles on children.

Eventually he said that surgery might be best.

This time Joey was to have 13 incisions between his groin and his feet, and he came home from the hospital in long leg casts. Matthew came to our home every morning and worked on Joey. He said that it's especially important to reconnect meridians after surgery. Whatever he did, even Joey's doctor remarked at how quickly Joe healed and his scars almost disappeared. If you hadn't witnessed it, you would have said a miracle occurred!

I am forever indebted to Matthew and his wisdom in healing – for myself and my son.

Matthew helped me in other ways as well. He taught me about "balance". He taught me that when one area of our lives is out of balance, it affects other areas. For example, when one works too many hours at a job, then home life will suffer. And if one is spending all one's energy to nurture others, then the well-being of oneself will suffer.

This applies to mothers and fathers. How different would parenting be if fathers could pull back on business hours and spend more time in the home. And how different would parenting be if mothers had the support from "a village" for this most important work.

Which leads me to say that you can't have too many mothers and conscious fathers! I remember telling my friends that they had permission to parent my children in my absence. Our children need our 'collective care'.

When I look back over my own life, I have always had another "mother" in my life. Probably more.
I have had guidance and support from other women, even when I moved to California. Today, we might call them "mentors", but the point is that we are never unaided in our journeys. All of Life supports our travels.

I Have Become My Mother

I suspect that every woman says to herself that she won't do or say things she disliked in her own mother. Now I believe that this 'friction' that arises with our parents is just Life's way of preparing us to live our lives on our own terms. We test those beliefs we grew up with; we sort through which ones we'll keep and which we won't.

I remember the first time I acknowledged 'becoming my mother'. My husband now worked early in the morning. It was my birthday. This day I fell back into a deep sleep after he left for work at 5:30 a.m. I was awakened by the phone ringing. It was my neighbor across the street telling me my boys had just walked past her house. OMG! I jumped out of bed and as I was pulling on clothes the phone rang again. This time it was my neighbor down the street. My boys had rung her bell wanting to know if her girls could play. They were there on her front stoop in their pajamas! I told her I'd be right there and ran out my door to retrieve them. I actually carried one under each arm back to the house, all the while asking them what were they thinking? What were they doing at 6:30 in the morning leaving the house?? I sat them down at our dining table and asked if this was their idea of a 'birthday gift' to me.

Yes, I was laying on the guilt. And then it hit me –
I HAD BECOME MY MOTHER! And I saw clearly how my sons were just like my brothers and I remembered how my mother was forever retrieving them from the next block. After I finished ranting and raving, my son Joe very calmly said "Mom, why are you so upset? We looked both ways before we crossed the street."

And then I knew!..........Oh dear God, give me strength and courage.

***

And later on, when my boys were older Joey also said something profound to me. He said "Mom, there's no pleasing you." It stopped me dead in my tracks. Yes, I had become my mother in more ways than one. Please understand, I'm not blaming her. I'm seeing clearly the behaviors we grow up with that, unless challenged, will continue. He was right. Critical parents yield critical children who grow up to be critical parents – and so it goes.

I determined then and there to break that habit. It begins with first – accepting ourselves, flaws and all.
And that's OK.

We are not meant to be perfect. We are meant to be loving. And when we are loving, everything is perfect.

As Louise Hay says "we are perfectly imperfect".
I know my parents wanted the best for me – truly, they tried with what means they had. I also know that we are an evolving species and we take what we know and add to it to produce new ideas, innovations, discoveries, etc. (Actually, this is what Fibonacci discovered, and it's a wonderful pattern to practice.)
Actually, this is how we grow!

***

Joey was to give me another aha moment. One night we were arguing over something and Joe turned to me and said "Mom, love ALL of me – for the part that is challenging you is the part that is teaching you."

I remember those words because at that moment I knew I heard TRUTH and I said to my son "wait" and I went and wrote down those words so I would never forget them or the Wisdom they conveyed.

It IS the challenges that grow us, change us, move us forward. I knew then and there that to embrace ALL of Life is the Work. The gifts are in the dark *and* in the light.

So often, we 'set up' our lives. We get the right job, marry the right person, live in the right house in the right town. And then we want to "freeze" that frame and not move from it. And so often, just when that happens and we are feeling like we made it, some thing or someone steps in and blows it all to hell.

I would bet that not many can say they have the life they exactly planned. I certainly haven't. I remember telling my mother that "it was *my* life, and in the end I would be responsible and answer for it."

I've learned to take the 'judgement' out of events.
I've learned to say that "everything happens for my good". There's a blessing in everything! I can say that now because I've lived it. I can say also that while everything happens for our good, not everything *feels* good. That's because some events rip open our hearts, change the course of our lives, prune our thinking and our beliefs, open our eyes to see clearly.

Yes, I have become my mother – the best of my mother! I had the right mother. And the right father.
And siblings as well. I'm grateful to all of them – now that I see them clearly.

***

When Eddie was very little he asked me "Momma, when is tomorrow?" "Well" I said, "you go to sleep and when you wake up, it's tomorrow." So the next morning when he awoke he asked "is it tomorrow?"

"No, it's today." I said. And this continued for a couple of days. And finally he said one morning "it's *this* day". I wasn't to get that lesson for quite a while. He was so right. There's only *this* day. It's the only day we have. And you know the rest: yesterday is gone and tomorrow isn't here. There is only the 'present'.

This was to be such a gift! How often did we hear "wait until you grow up!" As if then and only then would Life begin for us.

Today, when I see parents with young babies, my advice is to cherish the time and be in the moment with their young ones. "This too shall pass" applies to the sleepless nights, the diaper stages, the potty-training stages, etc. but the time is so short that children are little and innocent. Being "present" is the best gift!

THIS DAY

This day can be all I dream
This day can be more that it seems
A day unlike any other before
This day – let it be – this day
This day can unfold in no ordinary way
This day can be bold when I stand and behold
The wonder of that Great Designer's hands
To hold Eternity – the beginning and the end
Who knows without a shadow of a doubt
That I will find my way…this day
Oh, let me love like that!
Let me open up 'til I'm all filled up
with joy and peace and You always here.
This day I pray, this day I say
This day is the day my dreams come to me
This day – oh let it be!

11-15-2000
LD

Later, when Eddie was in the 4th grade he told me one day "Mom, you know that voice you hear inside you? Well, you don't hear it anymore when you get to the 4th grade."

I pondered that for a long time. Maybe it's the Divine Plan. Maybe, at that time in their lives children begin to relate 'outside' themselves. They lose that inner guidance.

I call that inner guidance Intuition and I always listened to mine. Except when I wanted to 'fit in'.
I know what I knew was different from what I saw.
So when Eddie confided this to me, I understood what he was feeling. I also knew it was important for me to tell him to 'keep listening'.

You see, intuition is our Higher Power guiding us.
I knew when I listened to mine and when I ignored it.
I didn't know it was my God talking to me until I was nearly 40 years old! But I had the good sense to realize that God was showing me through my children what patterns to let go of, and what patterns to adopt universally.

And I keep listening............

I will share another gift Eddie was to give me….

When my boys were 5 and 3 I took a job as a sales representative for gift lines. My territory was small and I could work from home, and work around my life. Joe was in kindergarten at the local public school and Eddie went to Kindercare three days a week. I had the assistance of my mother-in-law as well. Joe had school half a day and then the Kindercare bus would pick him up to spend the afternoon there. Generally I would pick them both up around 5 p.m. when my work day was done.

I suspect Eddie was on the lookout for me, because he always seemed to see me first when I came through the door. His whole face would light up and he would run to me with open arms. It made me forget my own day and become fully present to this joyful child. It made me realize that I was a mother first – and my children needed my 'presence', but I also needed theirs. Here was 'unconditional Love' coming right at me! A gift almost too big to acknowledge!!

My husband worked nights and was not home for dinner, but dinner-time was a ritual in our house.
And one thing I learned was that children *love* candlelight…. especially boys. I would light candles and a "hush" would fall over the table. Everyone whispered – the noise level went way down. And as we ate dinner we each got to talk about our day.
This sharing of food and time is so important! *Everyone* got to share.

I remember from my own childhood how important the Sunday dinner ritual was. It was important for all the family to be there. There wasn't the communication then – all voices important to share – but the ritual was important – coming together.

Today, it's not easy to get a family together. Our "making ends meet" has driven many to work schedules that separate the family. This is where extended family comes in – the 'village' it takes to raise a child. Let's revisit the rituals that put our children first and that means putting family first.

I'm sorry to say that my husband was a man who worked long hours when we first had our children.

As I was learning about 'balance' I could see the patterns that contribute to imbalance in our society.

"Proving our worth" for men too, creates gross imbalances. Men are expected to spend many hours at their jobs – they are the breadwinners. But how many jobs allow for men to also be present for their children and families? If raising children became our "collective work" how would work patterns change?

One of the most important things I learned as a mother: I would no longer make a decision without thinking of another human being, namely my child. My life is forever altered – in a good way! I don't know too many men who realize this.

And one more thing I learned from my kids...............

In business we are always on a schedule. We are expected to show up on time. My work day was quite varied and oftentimes I would be late to pick up my children, either from school or child care. I slowly realized that they were just as important as my job – and they were counting on me to be on time – to trust that I would do what I said I would do.

Being on time is an issue of respect!

Yes, we can be flexible, and today, with cell phones, we can text ahead. It doesn't change the behavior.

Be on time! It follows the thinking that makes adults accountable for what they say – especially to their children. Because our children are watching, and they are most definitely listening. And they most especially deserve our respect!

IN THE CLASSROOM

One of the greatest joys for me was to assist in my children's classrooms. I went back to work when Joey was 5 and Eddie was 3. My work allowed me to 'work' around my life. I could 'block out' the time I was to spend in the classroom. I know this was a gift, as so many working mothers do not have that luxury.

What I found is that when you have children you revisit everything you learned growing up!

When my children entered school my husband and I would often have conversations about our own schooling, and we both came to the conclusion that if you loved to read, you would do well in school. I was a sponge for information and read books since I was a young child. I loved learning! My husband didn't like reading. He found school tedious and difficult.

When it came to our children, he was content to let the teachers teach. Being in my children's classrooms gave me a different viewpoint. Being in my children's classrooms would also give me the opportunity to be observant – to again see what works and what doesn't and to make different choices.

Mulitple Intelligence

My children led me to attend classes in Multiple Intelligences at the University of Riverside.

I was led to these classes by the good people at Danbury School in Claremont. My son Joe had just finished a year struggling with his teacher. Here was a gifted child falling through the cracks. It had been a control issue the entire year. Someone had given me a book called HOW YOUR CHILD IS SMART by Dawna Markova. It gives a way to test your child and Joey was in the "leader of the pack" group. His label of cerebral palsy led many teachers to believe he was mentally challenged too, but this was clearly not the case. My frustration led me to take classes in Multiple Intelligence. I remember showing up the first day – me and 75 teachers from around the country. They asked why I was there. "Aren't parents a child's first teacher?" I asked.

Multiple Intelligence is the theory proposed by Howard Gardner of Harvard that children learn in many different ways. Schools traditionally teach to just two of those ways – linguistic and logical-mathematical – and if your child isn't dominant in those two intelligences they can become frustrated, bored and even check out of the whole learning process itself.

Dr. Sue Teele, the Director of the Institute of the Study of Multiple Intelligences (MI) when I attended said "All children can learn, but not in the same way, and not on the same day."

I attended classes during the summer months.

Laura D. Distarce

The teachers that attended would go back to their classrooms in the fall and implement these learning techniques. Since I didn't have a classroom, I assessed both my children's MI and brought the results to their teachers at the beginning of the school year.

What I learned is that my children learn differently from each other. To begin, Joey was audio and Eddie was visual. So I could recite times tables with Joe while doing dishes and he would get them. Joe heard me even when he wasn't looking right at me. With Ed, I had to write them out so he would see them and then he could learn them. I used to say "talking to Ed was like talking to a wall" – audio was not his first channel. I too am visual and realized that's why I can write out a list and then forget it – seeing it was enough to commit it to my memory.

I realized how important reading was and read to both my children – even in the womb!

I continued to read to my boys at night before bedtime. Joe loved being read to – he was audio. Ed and I were visual and Ed would read along with me and follow the words on the page. Often, Joe would laugh at a passage in the book that I would have to re-read to get its meaning.

Assessing their learning styles was the tool that enabled them, their teachers and me (parents) to facilitate learning.
Sadly, classrooms are so large and understaffed that teachers cannot devote time to such individual styles. But just knowing about these different ways of learning is invaluable.

What I learned is that when children aren't honored for the way they learn, they can resort to 'fight or flight' modes of behavior. This is the 'survivor' brain. Learning does not take place here. Learning takes place when children feel safe; when they are honored for who they are, as they are. They actually show us **how** they learn – if we would only take the time to observe them, listen, and realize **how** they are smart. We will understand how uniquely gifted all of our children are.

The better news is that teachers, parents **and** children can understand how the child processes information to facilitate learning. My sons were different. I sensed that but now I had better understanding of just how they learned and so did they! Clarity is a great tool. Diversity is key. Children perceive differences but they don't judge them. It is the teachers that must be clear so that all children can learn.

While attending classes in Mulitple Intelligence I was exposed to new understanding of just how the brain works.

In very simplistic terms the brain is a "pattern maker". It collects data from our experiences and forms a pattern – a program based on those experiences. We are products of our experiences as much as of our DNA. When the patterns accumulate the brain creates a "program", which will run automatically. It's these "programs" that we must question, and in truth, asking a question will 'interrupt' the program.........Do I believe this? Do I want to continue this? Is this TRUE? We can make a conscious effort to re-pattern and re-program our brains.

It was at one of these classes that I head Joel Barker, a futurist speak. One of the most profound things he talked about was Change. He talked about systems (patterns/programs) being "open" or "closed". He said in a "closed" system there is no room for change. He talked about 'change agents' coming from outside a system. The reason for this was that those **in** the system (the pattern/program) were indoctrinated in that system and would follow the rules of that system.

He talked of the "change agent" as a messenger – to be invited or resisted.

He talked about people who live in homogenous societies know only their own patterns.

He talked of the need for being an "open-ended" system – to continue to learn, to grow, to search for new experience.

What I also learned through the study of Multiple Intelligence is that the "being there" experience is the best teacher. It has the most impact on a child's education.

What I learned is that money is a tool for giving children that "being there" experience. All our children deserve that.

We don't stop learning because we are adults. We don't stop becoming. "Be ye transformed by the renewing of your minds." It's an ongoing process.

"Children: teach your parents well."

***

One of my childhood friends, whose children were a little older brought a program to her school called "Making Friends with Great Masters". I loved art, my son Eddie was showing signs of being a great artist, and I thought this program might be good at their school. So I brought it to the school and it was adopted. Another parent gratefully underwrote the cost of the program and we gathered volunteers to teach it in the classroom once a month. We would contrast great artists' work, showing different styles, etc. The children would come to understand what makes for great art and learn about the artists as well.

What we all learned is that many "great" artists did not do well in school. And we also learned that ART is quite subjective as to its "greatness".

And then the children would have a 'project'.
This was always the fun part. In the beginning, I was somewhat rigid about the art project – giving the children all kinds of parameters and guidelines. As the course progressed I began to see that when left alone to use their own imaginations, the children produced far more creative outcomes. This of course helped me at home as well. I still have Eddie's first project that he did in the 2nd grade. He brought home a pastel picture with four squares on the page. It was "a baseball field the way Monet would have painted it". And when he learned that there were original Monet paintings at the Norton Simon Museum, not far from where we lived, he insisted on seeing them.

I have on my piano framed pictures of my sons and my family. I also have something Eddie said at age 7.
It was the result of a conversation we were having about the Great Masters and artists in general. He turned to me and said:

"Nothing can draw like Life."

It's a profound and true statement. And it reminds me to *trust* Life with all its ups and downs. It's rich with experience needing only to be embraced fully.

My studies in Multiple Intelligence also introduced me to Jon Pearson, who presented at one of my classes. He walked into class talking to an imaginary dinosaur named Buck. (see I still remember!) He had Buck sit down and all during the class he kept referring to Buck, describing what Buck was wearing and commenting on what

Buck was saying. I laughed the entire day! He was a cross between Robin Williams and Jonathan Winters and he truly 'unleashed' the child in me. He taught using icons – pictures that represented the history lesson he wished to convey. It was a day that still lives in my memory all these years later. Learning can be fun! And children can have fun learning!

I wanted to incorporate what I had learned from Jon into the art lesson I was giving the next week in my son's classroom. So I had an idea. When I entered the classroom I motioned my 'imaginary friend' to sit on a stool by the front blackboard. I was talking to her and watched as the students began to regard me with question. "Oh" I said "let me introduce Luisa."

(I was totally 'winging this' but I thought – they don't know that – let's go with this! I knew the children would catch on and be spontaneous.) So I proceeded to describe what Luisa was wearing and told them she was French and a very good friend of mine who had come to visit and wanted to meet the students.

"She's wearing a big, black hat and a black dress with blue flowers, long white gloves, very high heels and long strands of pearls around her neck." During my art presentation I would often refer to Luisa and have conversation like she was really in the room. The students loved it! We were studying George Seurat's A Sunday Afternoon and pointillism (the technique he used).

After the lesson we would typically have a project for the children. "What?" I said to Luisa "oh, OK, I'll ask them." "So class, Luisa said for your project, she'll sit very still and you can draw her in pointillism."

The class cheered! So I described again what she was wearing, passed out the paper and markers and the kids got to work.

"What color are her eyes?" one child asked. All together, they shouted "blue". "What color is her hair?" another child asked. All together they shouted "brown". THEY SAW HER! (Just so you know I am a brown eyed blonde.) These children blew me away! I was flying by the seat of my pants and they got it!

I brought her back occasionally and even the next year when I again taught the art class. By this time I had the students telling me what Luisa was wearing and one student even said she had a big diamond ring on her finger. "Luisa, you got engaged?"
After that class one young student came up to me and whispered in my ear "I have an imaginary friend too."
Wow, was Luisa my 'alter-ego'? Who knows, who cares! Those students had fun! I had fun! Learning can be fun! Learning should be engaging.

Computers have changed the way children learn. Children no longer have to memorize facts and dates and then remember them for testing. We live in the information age. Children learn how to access information, become critical thinkers and most importantly, connect what they learn to their own lives and others. Above all else, children must understand the relevance of what they learn.

Parents are children's first teachers. Many had less than perfect educational experiences themselves. They believe leaving the teaching to teachers is best.
I believe that when everyone is involved in a child's learning then it becomes a win/win situation.
I relearned things in geography and science and history that I had forgotten! In Truth, we should all be life-long students – always learning and growing.

I learned that the "being there experience" is the best way a child learns. Exposing children to art, culture, theater, dance, music at an early age creates a life-long patron. These are the things that make our lives rich, whether we are 'on stage' or in the audience.

Sadly, these are the things that are going away for our children.

I realize our education system keeps trying. They know we lag behind in math and science compared to other countries. What I experienced when my boys were in school was that teachers taught to testing. The testing was everything. What I learned from Multiple Intelligence was that some kids don't test well on tests. If given verbally, they would score much higher. So testing can be misleading – it doesn't give the whole measure of a child's intelligence.

Dr. Teele often remarked that the one-room schoolhouse of yesteryear was the best schoolroom.
They taught reading, writing and arithmetic. Coincidently, those were skills drummed into me in parochial school. We read; we wrote; learned sentence structure and spelling. We memorized our times tables. All these skills I've used all my life.
And regardless of the computer age, so will my children and their children.

When I attended the Institute of the Study of Multiple Intelligence in 1995, Howard Gardner had identified seven intelligences: spatial, logical-mathematical, bodily-kinesthetic, interpersonal, intrapersonal, linguistic and musical.

What Gardner and the Institute suggested was rather than 'label' our children with these learning styles, we simply identify the dominant ones that facilitate learning, and possibly improve on the less dominant ones to create a complete atmosphere for learning.... *all* children's needs met.

Afterwards, Gardner added an eighth intelligence:

natural (and subsequently, two more). Having the knowledge of Multiple Intelligences made it easier for me to recognize how children learned, whenever and wherever I was with them.

I helped out in Eddie's 5th grade classroom. I would take on a struggling student and give them the extra help they might need to get a math concept or understand grammar when writing. I noticed that many of these students didn't get sentence structure and I asked the teacher when would they learn to diagram a sentence. The teacher didn't know! So I asked if I could demonstrate it to the class and the teacher agreed. Wow, I learned diagraming sentences in the 4th grade! These students couldn't write a sentence because they hadn't learned about structure and so I explained it to them, recalling the hours I spent on this very thing.

I also observed how the teacher reacted with the students. He often yelled at them until their eyes glazed over and they checked out. He often asked me how I related so well and I told him about his yelling and that kids don't respond to that. He meant well. I too was taught by teachers that instilled fear into us.
I learned because I was afraid not to. But I had come to learn that children learn best in a nurturing environment – just like at home. Teachers are people too. They bring their own "patterns" to the classroom…..some good, some not so good. Schools must be "safe" environments for all children.

And so should the World………….

Random Acts of Kindness

When Eddie told me that it's in 4th grade (or there about) that you don't hear that 'voice' anymore I began to observe the behaviors of the students in the 4th and 5th grade. There were the bullies on the playground and competition between the girls.

At that same time I had been exposed to Random Acts of Kindness and I brought it to the school as something we might honor and do. There was great resistance from the teachers. They saw it as one more thing to add to their load. I saw it as a way for the children to reach out.

I will tell you that the one thing I know is that as a parent, you can't tell your children what they should do if you don't do it as well. I was reading about Random Acts of Kindness and I remember the day I decided to "pay it forward" as it is also referred to.

I decided when I stopped for coffee that I would pay for the person behind me. "Random" doesn't mean you don't think about what you will do. So this particular day there was a long line. "OK, I'm going to do this." I said to myself. When I got up to the counter I whispered to the waitress "I'm paying for the person behind me." She didn't hear me. "Speak up" she said. By now I was holding up the line, so I repeated it again – this time louder.

The person behind me was a man – a sheriff in uniform. So I turned to him and in a louder voice I said "I'm buying you coffee today. It's not a come-on, it's just what I want to do." He was quite surprised, but didn't say anything. I paid for my coffee and his and went out to my car. I did it!

I don't know why it took such courage to do that. It was not a huge thing! I was so immersed in my own thought that I didn't notice the sheriff had come out and stood beside my car door. I rolled down my window and he said "thank you – you can't know how much that means to me". Really! What happens is that you see that you have the power to make or break someone's day. Actually, he made *my* day!

I also remember one night I was going to listen to music with some good friends. It had been raining for days and I pulled into the local market to get some cash. There was a man standing in front of the market who asked me if I could help him out with a few dollars. I had a couple of ones which I gave to him. Then I went to gas up my car, but that man would not leave my thoughts. Here I was, going to spend some money and time having fun. I didn't know what he would be doing. Was he homeless in this pouring rain? I drove back to the market and he was still there. I rolled down my window and asked him to come closer so we could speak. "What's happened to you?" I asked. He wanted to find a room to stay in for his wife and himself. He had a son who was with relatives. He was driving up North to pay off some tickets and was promised a job on his return. At that time $20 would secure a decent room.
So I gave him the money and I said "when you have found your way, pass it on please." And I also said that I hoped the rain would stop and he would have a safe journey. He thanked me sincerely. I will never know what he spent the money on. I only know that the next day bloomed clear and sunny as if in answer to my prayer and I thought 'thank you, God'.

What I realized from doing acts of kindness is that people have become so jaded that they are suspect to any kindness shown them. They have been conditioned to believe they live in an unfriendly world.

So being in my son's classroom gave me an idea.
I talked about Random Acts of Kindness to the children and I told them that since they were the oldest children in the school, they

could set the example on the playground. I told them how bullies really want attention, but they don't know how to get it in a positive way, so they get it in a negative way. I made them all "ambassadors of kindness" and told them, if they decided to take this on, then opportunities would come to them – they didn't have to seek them out – and they could decide on how they would respond. I told them that when there's a conflict, the real winner walks away – not in defeat, but in strength. And each time I visited the classroom, these students would relate their stories of kindness.

I remember one student asking: "what if you decide to be kind, and you do something nice, but the other person is still mean to you?" "Well" I said, "there are two things about that you need to understand."
"First: practice, practice, practice. Because, second:
It doesn't matter how they respond, it matters that *you* acted this way. And each time you practice, you will grow your own resolve that you can make a difference in the world."

And this is so true for those that say something like "they'll spend it on booze or cigarettes". Or worse.

I also remember one time around Christmas, my children and I were going into Target. Eddie had received $20 from his grandmother. We were approached by a man with his young child who was asking for a donation. In those days I carried very little cash with me and had none to give to the man.
But Eddie pulled out his $20 bill and asked me if he could give it to them. "It's yours to decide." I said.
He did give it to them! And because of his kindness, I gave Eddie $20 to spend on himself. That small act has stayed with me all these years and still swells my heart.

Let me repeat: Opportunities will always come to you so you can decide how to act. Many times when I am in my car I see people at freeway entrances asking for help. Whether I can give them something or not, I always ask for a blessing for them.

And second: It does not matter what that 'other' person does with the money. It matters that you acted.…..one small kindness at a time will help you see a little clearer.

I decided to create a book of the children's stories. I created pages for them to write or draw their own best experience of Random Acts of Kindness and I printed them up and put them into a book for each of them and for their library at school. I dedicated it to them and to all ambassadors of kindness. It's not a fad that's had its run. It's timeless and needed now more than ever. It empowered these children. They could make a difference. They could teach the world!

***

When my children went to middle school I still wanted to help in the classroom. I was told to "let go of my child". "Well then, give me a struggling student" I said. And they gave me children with special needs, who gathered in a windowless room with no heat. Unbelievable but true!

More importantly, I believe that middle school is the make or break time for children, especially boys. And it's the time schools need more support from parents. And schools should welcome that.

I think about something Joel Barker, the futurist, taught me. "There are closed systems and open systems. Closed systems are their own demise. Open systems leave room for growth, and usually that growth comes from outside the system."

Think on this. Each of us is like that system. We are closed or open – learning and growing – or not.

I have known for a long time that I am a 'change agent'. Change happens around me because I let it happen *to* me. Life is about change!

I think back to that time my children were in school.

It was the most beautiful time for *me*. To be able to be in the classroom is something I encourage every parent to do. I realize today that both parents may work. But if we don't claim our children as our BEST and MOST IMPORTANT work, then we will continue to deny them all that they can truly be. And too soon, they grow up. So we must claim this for our children and our children's children.

As Life would have it, I found myself in another classroom. It was a kindergarten class and the teacher of it seemed to me to embody that "natural" intelligence. She had been studying Multiple Intelligences as well and our meeting was synchronistic. She taught differently than I had ever experienced. At every chance, she had the children outdoors. She had been at this school for almost 35 years and had put in a nature trail, a garden, and before she retired, an orchard. She planted sunflowers and created a sunflower house for the children to sit inside for reading and learning. They learned to count by counting fava beans that grew in the garden. She had composts piles and worm farms and I remarked to her that she was creating "little environmentalists" out of these 5 year olds. Indeed she was! She knows who she is and I am privileged to have met her and still call her my friend.

Her classroom seemed a little haphazard to some, but she got the work done. I often helped her and marveled at how she organized her groups and facilitated the learning for her students. She always connected the dots – helped the children understand *why* they were learning about *what* they were learning. My strong suit was art, and so I gladly led the art projects. She had strong volunteer support from parents.

I truly wish my children could have had her for their teacher. She was dedicated to her profession and kept learning herself. I learned so much from her!

She taught about the food chain, and children could actually plant seeds, watch them grow and harvest them. She taught about recycling and preserving our earth through her nature trail and gardens. She called it 'garden-based' learning. Today I see on Facebook questions like "should we have gardens at children's school?" Absolutely! It's the best 'being there' experience a child can have!

It teaches a respect for our Mother Earth. It teaches the cycle of Life which is ongoing. It teaches preserve and protect, not conquer and destroy. It teaches community and working together for goals.

If Life began in a garden, I believe it's time to return to the garden. It's not so complicated. We've made it too complicated. Children have simple needs.

They don't need as much 'stuff' as we think. They need the basics, but more importantly, they need our focus and our attention.

What if *everyone's* job was to move our children forward? To create the environments that are safe for everyone's child. To create the schools that cater to all children's needs. To preserve places for them to play and explore. I've noticed that most towns will build housing over parks and so will most cities. We need both – a balance.

I've often heard that "digging in the dirt" is the best therapy. I know it's been true for me. Some children have never seen green pastures, oceans, fields of flowers. Some have never seen the night sky filled with stars.

In Nature is our pattern for Life. And each time we return to Nature we are renewed and made stronger by the pruning. We've lost our balance – children are the balance.

THE GARDEN IN MY HEART

There is a Garden in my Heart
Lush green and gentle slopes
Still water blue and deep
Beauty unsurpassed
Details left to God
Air rich with Peace and Joy
I breathe into my Being
Everywhere there is Love
Dazzling like diamonds
More precious than gold
This Garden in my Heart

And I share it all with you!
This song my soul sings
The music of the Angels
This child that dances in the Light
In the Garden of my Heart

LD

Never Say Never

I always believed that if I married and had children I would never get a divorce. My own parents divorced and I knew the pain it caused, though I understood why.

But we always say 'we will be different'. We believe that. And I don't believe that people who marry ever believe they will divorce – not when that union is filled with promise and hope. But Life happens, and not in ways we can predict. I found myself facing the need to separate from my husband. I realized that my children were seeing 'relationship' and they would form relationship based on what they saw. So after some years of anguish, I knew I had to make a change.

At that time my children were 7 and 9. It was not an easy decision and I prayed for guidance. One day my husband and I were arguing about where to live. I knew I wanted him to be in a good place. He was still the father of my children. If I stayed in the house we had, it would mean he would live in a room. The house represented struggle to me, and with working full time and being a mother, I knew I couldn't deal with the upkeep. I had learned long ago, when my childhood house burned, that things don't matter, so I was never attached to "things". I liked nice things, just like everyone else, but they held no great importance to me, and I also knew they could come and go and come back again.

Joey came into the kitchen and said "why don't you both live where my friend Josh lives". Josh lived with his grandparents, around the corner, in a townhouse development. I had dropped Joey off there to play with Josh, but I had never been through the complex. So after dinner, the boys and I took pen and paper and went to explore.

There were four townhomes for sale. One of them had a flyer that explained the size and price and I thought – we could do this! We could sell our home and buy townhomes and the boys could go back and forth between us.

(Did I mention I lived with 'wise men'?)

It was a perfect solution. I came home and told my husband "this can be a win/win solution". I contacted the real estate agents on the flyer and met with them. "This will happen" I told them, so if they had doubts they could bow out. Otherwise, I wanted to sell the house and buy the townhomes and be in by August so I could get my children settled for school. Even my husband had doubts, but I advised him that this was the best solution and to flow with it and not hold it up.

I have read that the Universe supports decisions. Well, I made the decision, and wow, the Universe stepped in..........we sold our home in 15 days in a very slow market! We bought the townhomes and moved in the beginning of August. What I didn't realize was that my children could stay in the same school system and walk to school as it was closer than where we lived before. AND the complex had lots of children their ages.

I used to remark that it was a new sitcom "Around the Corner" – because that's where my husband lived. My children had bedrooms in both homes and they could go back and forth and be with both of us. It was a great solution, whether it met with others' approval or not – it worked for us.

What I know is that children want to love their parents – no matter how that parent is – they come from unconditional Love, and they remind us – for we have forgotten.

When my children went to school that fall, I told their teachers of our separation. One teacher remarked about my "needy little child".

I had to remind her that some children live with both parents and still they are needy children. My children knew they were loved, no matter where their parents lived. I had to remind them of that often.

I know that people mean well, but it's human nature to take sides and I felt it keenly in the community in which I lived and my own circle of friends.

What I know is that we all do better with love and support. When I think back on that time, I realized that I kept focused on raising my children. Yes, it was more difficult since I was a single, working Mom.

I remember changing jobs and in the interview I said "I'm a mother first." It was to be the only time I heard "that's as it should be."

COMMUNICATION

When my husband and I separated, I remember someone trying to give me good advice regarding our children. They said we needed to focus on them and continue to communicate regarding their well-being. I know they meant well, but the thought occurred to me that if we were communicating we'd most likely still be married! It seems to me that communication is what it's all about. Even when we watch movies, aren't we telling the couple on the screen who are about to go their separate ways: "hey you guys, you just need to talk to each other". It's clear to us what the problem is, but then we are a little removed. Not so emotionally involved. Not actually in it.

We need to step back a bit from our own lives, and take a broader view, a longer look at what works and what doesn't. We do have emotions, and we are meant to feel – to feel happy, to feel honored and respected, to feel joy. No one doesn't want to feel these emotions.

Feelings are important, and how we feel is not about 'right or wrong', it's more about honestly communicating. We don't communicate well, and we deny feelings.

So at the recommendation of someone I trusted, I took a communication class with my two children and their father, my ex-husband. It was an eight-week class and there were about fifty people in the class comprising a variety of family situations – from single parents with children to married parents with adopted children – all needing to relearn communication skills.

The first half of the class we, the parents, were separated from our own children. We got to listen to other parents' and other children's experiences as we learned about the fundamentals for true communication. Our children also got to hear experiences other than their own. No one judged anyone else, as everyone was there because they admitted communication, or rather lack of it, was hurting everyone in the family.

In the second half of the evening, we were reunited with our own children, and got to do some exercises in the new skills we were learning. The hope was that when the classes ended we would have some good guidelines for what promoted good communication. The hope was that, with practice, we could implement these new skills into effective communication.

During one session the instructor showed us a model of the parent/child roles in terms of "control" and communication.

* In infancy, the parents have total control of the child's welfare.
* During adolescence, the control is "shared".
* When the child reaches adulthood, they hopefully have reached the stage where they are independent and empowered to make their own choices (hopefully ones that serve them).

This made so much sense to me: Parents as guiding forces in children's lives.

When the instructor asked the adults in the class how many of them grew up with this model only one could say that his parents followed that model. The other adults admitted that their parents had full control – full say – until the child left home. How many can relate to having parents that made most of their choices for them? "Shared" control comes down to communicating. No one communicated very well back then.

If our parents were making all our choices for us then we weren't getting much practice. No wonder when we left home, we fell flat on our faces!

When it came to life-altering choices we were unprepared. We did what we were told to do. No matter how talented anyone is they still need to practice. Children that don't have some say in their choices don't get to practice.

There are people that will argue that children need rules; that, in fact, Society cannot run without rules and chaos would ensue without definite guidelines. Rebellion occurs because people won't follow the rules. The mal-content.

In Truth, what's happening is that people "battle" when they are not honored or seen, when their voices are not heard. They battle against an institution, a system that says there is only one way to do things. They battle just to be heard. Another voice, a different viewpoint. They battle, because not too many people learned how to communicate. All these 'patterns' that play out as adults were learned while they were children.

Go back to the model on communication: during adolescence the control is "shared". That means parents have a voice (all parents), and children have a voice. This is where communication becomes communication. It is two way. It is "shared" voices. Of course it's easier for one person to give the directives and everyone else follows them. But that is an old paradigm, and we know that it does not serve everyone.

Choices are what we want our children to become comfortable with, and practicing can begin as soon as they have a preference. Small choices – like what clothes to wear, what restaurant to eat in. This might seem trivial to many adults. Many believe that children shouldn't be given choices at all. That children don't know what's good for them. I wholeheartedly disagree.

I once heard a neuro-biologist being interviewed on the radio. She said some very interesting things about babies and how they develop. Babies, she said, needed space to move about freely, not the restrictive environment of a carseat. Their brains needed their bodies moving freely to grow and develop. She also suggested that the "terrible two's" were just the child mirroring back the amount of "control" the parent was exerting over them.

One of the most valuable pieces of information I learned regarding communication is this: sarcasm is not conducive to clear communication. It is not honest. And oftentimes we mask our true meaning behind a sarcastic retort. We're not really sure of the other party's intent. I remember my son Eddie remarking to me from the back seat of the car: "Mom, are you being sarcastic?" He started to ask me that right after the classes we took.

Sarcasm is for late-night shows or comedy skits, but it's not for clear and honest communication.

***

We hear the word "paradigm" quite a lot today. I believe some words become so clichéd that they lose their value. The word paradigm means pattern.

Here's a paradigm that has been prevalent in our society. It is a "dominator" model where the father is at the top and the mother and children below him. Most adults today probably grew up in that pattern. The "control" is at the top. Roles were well defined. Fathers knew theirs, mothers and children knew theirs. In Truth, a woman could also be at the top, but again, it's a pattern based on one person in control and the communication is in the form of a directive from the top.

In just fifty years, I have seen roles, once so rigidly defined, break down, or more correctly, break open – shatter – to allow a more expanded definition.
There are a lot of people who feel the world is worse for this. Everyone was much more comfortable when we knew our roles. People liked things the way they were. But, truthfully, *some* people were more comfortable, and only *some* people liked things the way they were.

Having grown up in New Jersey, and now living as many years and more in California, I can see a big difference in the mindsets of these opposite shores. The mindset I grew up in was largely one of very well defined rules and roles. Rules ruled! Traditions were embedded in our psyches…what to think, what to wear, what to do. Fairly rigid mindsets, slow to change. You fit into it, and if you didn't, you moved……out! (and in my case - west)

When I moved to California at the age of 24, I realized just how narrow my experiences had been. Here there were no rules, or less rules, something very foreign to me. A slower, more casual pace. In fact, it was liberating. There wasn't the "judgement" that seemed to accompany every move I made growing up. No one seemed to mind much how I lived.

Wisely, someone I met soon after moving to California told me that it took a few years to acclimate, but that the longer people stayed, the more they liked it. My own opinion today is that people are "drawn" to California to find themselves. That in a place where anything goes, one has to decide for oneself what one values. All those choices can seem overwhelming, especially when you are not used to making choices at all. But it is only in the atmosphere of free choice that you hone yourself. Your choices are your own, and you learn to own them, knowing you are defining yourself by them. And re-defining yourself, for Life is about change. When I was a little girl I heard that "only unhappy people change". The status-quo was firmly planted. The mindsets were 'set'. And so were we all. Life dealt us our hand and we lived with it, and some would just have to make due.

Much has changed. Many blame it on the women's movement, and I marvel at how women truly do get dumped on in this world. Things needed to change. And things will change again as more find their voices.

The family unit seems to be falling apart. Is it falling apart because the old structure doesn't honor every member of the family? Is it shattering – to expand into greater definition of what comprises family?

Statistics tell us that half of all marriages end in divorce. I am not the only one who believes marriages are breaking up because the old structure of marriage is dysfunctional. Marriage is meant to be a partnership – an equal partnership. Family is also a partnership – with all members having equal value and voices.

When children become teenagers, all hell can break loose in a household. That goes with the territory, or so we're told. They are wanting some say in their lives. Of course, teenagers will argue that they deserve total say, but parents willing to share control can give them a voice and still have the final say if agreement can't be reached. When family members learn to communicate before they reach that stage, things could go a lot smoother. One-way communication does not take into consideration the other's viewpoint. It's not a dialogue, it's a debate that often escalates into heated and oftentimes physical battles. Debates historically have only one winner.

I believe that true communication is new terrain for everyone. Communicating for understanding honors everyone's voices, even if they disagree. True communication strives for win-win outcomes.

The communication class taught us something else: 'anger' is just the tip of the iceberg. It masks the real emotions that are hiding just beneath the surface. No one can deny that we are an angry society. The anger stems from distinctly different sources, but it meets at the top of that iceberg – and it literally freezes all of us, and keeps us frozen, or more correctly, paralyzed.

Anger unchecked leads to violence. And there's no denying we live in a violent society. But we have condoned this violence. We have distanced ourselves from our true feelings. We're numb. We're operating on remote. I wonder sometimes if we are willing to let the violence continue because we cannot acknowledge the absence of *love* in our lives. That in this great country of ours that has so much, our lives are filled up with things, but the emptiness we feel could sink the Titanic.

The antidote? Children
Why? Because children are Joy, and will show us ours, if we let them. Children can remind us of that lost child within ourselves that needs nurturing, that has hidden behind walls of ignorance, isolation, separation, and pain. Spending time with children can cure us.

There might be missed opportunities we lament about as adults. Hindsight is perfect, and we let it beat us up, or rather into submission that offers no possibility of success. It is never too late to make a choice, a different choice – one that could bring a different way to be, to live, and even feel good!

There are many ways to begin – here's just one:

I truly believe that if every adult spent at least a half-hour coloring we would have a lot less angry people on the road and at the office. We would begin the "thaw" so necessary to get back to what truly matters. Go on, try it, you might like it! And this time – no one is watching to see if you stay inside the lines.

I even dare you to take your coloring books to work!

(I wrote this 15 years ago, but I see that today coloring has become an 'adult' hobby. Hooray!)

A LIFE WORTH LIVING

What if we just stopped all that behavior that makes us have to prove our worth. How would we be? How would we move through life? How many have honestly examined their own patterns, their own belief systems? An unexamined life is no life, it is just existence. There's a difference.

Children watch adults very closely. They look to adults for protection. They deserve a world where they feel safe. We all deserve that. And ALL our children deserve that.

I know what it is to feel afraid. I felt afraid for the first 15 years of my life. And I lived in the suburbs, in a nice community, my parents realizing the American Dream. I should have enjoyed all the benefits that "dream" offered. To some extent I did - having a safe neighborhood in which to play, attending good schools. But we lived in a very 'homogenous' town, and, in part, I was protected but naive. Many of us were from European heritage. I was from Irish/German/Italian heritage – we were referred to as "mutts". Even though everyone was "white", there was an undercurrent of mistrust. There was a "stick with your own kind" attitude and it spilled over into our religious faiths as well. My upbringing did not protect me from the mistrust I would learn about - later, when I moved out into the world. That "dream" was only for some - and it was that "dream" that Dr. Martin Luther King referred to in his Work - that ALL God's children enjoy that dream. All God's children live free from fear.

***

It wasn't until my own children were dabbling in drugs, when I was seeking help for them, that my eyes were opened and my ears could hear. All rehabilitation programs had to be directed by the Courts, and that meant they had to get arrested first. It was then, and only then that I realized how mothers living in the inner cities must feel..........and I cried - for them! And I was ashamed. That we haven't been listening. That we haven't seen that the violence is a cry from the soul. How does that mother send her child off to school each morning I wondered? How do they manage? Empathy is the ability to put oneself in another's shoes, and try to experience what they would be going through. Yes, most times we don't understand until the problem lands in our own laps.

We ignored the drug problems in our country until they traveled 'uptown'. Then, and only then, did we bring the problem to the forefront. The wealthy could keep their children out of jail. They could send them to fancy rehabilitation centers. Today, everyone is affected by drugs - in every community across our nation - especially in the wealthier ones.

It is Gary Zukav who rightly said "all addiction is about not wanting to feel". So what does it say that even in the wealthiest communities in our country, there are gross addictions – drugs, alcohol, etc. Having "more" isn't the answer. *Love* is the answer.

What I've come to realize is that LOVE is not an emotion – it is creative energy of the Most High Source – or what many call God. It is what we come from and what we are made of. God IS Love – Creative energy that brought into manifestation our Universe and the earth we live on. At Its Source it is invisible – we only see the effect of its Cause....

The following is a piece I wrote to bring clarity and understanding to my question: what is Love?

THIS THING CALLED LOVE

I wish to write about this 'thing called Love' – this phenomenon. What IS it?

Certainly our History has shown that we are most occupied with defining it. It's the subject of poetry, songs, books, movies and relationships.

I don't think I'm the only one who is confused about this thing called LOVE. There are so many conflicting messages out there. I'll give you just a couple of examples. I remember a best-selling book that was made into a movie. It was called LOVE STORY.

Remember the line "Love means never having to say you're sorry."? How many of us bought into that line? Ah yes, people would say, and nod their heads as if they completely understood its meaning. I wondered "how come I don't get it?" To me, that line was an invitation for Abuse, with a capital "A".

Or this: Every time I hear Tina Turner sing "what's love got to do with it?" I have this conversation: "Tina, what does that mean? Can someone tell me what that means?"

I'd be talking back to the radio "doesn't Love have EVERYTHING to do with it?"

I do know this: if everyone were really honest, they would agree: Everyone wants to love and be loved – everyone! Love is not just for the lucky – Love is for everyone.

No matter what else we think we are doing on this planet – we are all here learning and remembering how to love – ourselves and each other. No matter what you think your job is, your status is, where you live, dark-skinned, light-skinned, male, female, child, adult, believer, atheist – we are all on the same page! We didn't come here to figure out anything else. There are no more secrets. There is no longer any reason to be afraid.

We came here to experience Love. God wanted us to experience perfect Love, but first we had to know what imperfect love was about. We came here to experience God. So we had to know what God is and what God isn't. So maybe our separation from our Source *was* Divinely planned. God gave us free will. I wonder if God ever wanted to rethink that one.... "What was I thinking!" NO, God would have to give us free will, or we couldn't be free. And above all else God wishes for us all to be free. I sometimes have a thought that God is saying "They are taking this all too seriously – they have bought into the drama! LIGHTEN UP!" I hear God saying. "Don't they understand that their life is like a movie? They are the star, they are also the director, the producer, the casting agent, heck, they're writing the script! When will they get tired of the movie they're in? Don't they know that if they don't like the script, they can rewrite it, if they don't like the supporting actors, they can re-cast those roles? I'M GETTING TIRED OF WATCHING RE-RUNS! Please make another movie!" And then God says "I'll even give them a hand; they only have to ask."

TRUTH is, Pain is serious business, especially when we're in it. But greater TRUTH is, pain is our Joy in another reflection.....and our pain is meant to be moved through. And we'll be in pain, until we're not. We must not be so hard on ourselves. We've all been confused and confounded by this thing called LOVE.

So.....God set us on this journey to LOVE, holding us all in the embrace of perfect Love, and letting us go, to find our way back, knowing the outcome was assured.

God was there all the time, we were looking elsewhere, blinded by the glitter, the power, the stuff we thought if we just had we'd be happy and *then* we'd be loving. We all thought that at one time or another – or one lifetime or another. We also were taught that – in the very places we believed we could trust....home, Church. But the Truth is, in separating from God, we also separated from ourselves and each other. So the journey to Love is also a journey to wholeness – Oneness.

Our problems as they manifest today may have various expressions, but they all stem from the same 'root cause' – separation from God. Our **false** belief that we are separated from God – our Source. When we understand that that can never happen, then we understand that the same Godstuff in all of us connects us to each other – and we begin to see with new eyes, clearly, holistically, and holy – for it is a Divine sight to behold. And you know what that is – it's LOVE. Because just as God IS – LOVE IS. And it's standing right in front of us, and all around us.

So what can I tell you of this thing called Love? Well, it's been pretty distorted. No wonder we don't recognize it anymore, or give it the honor and praise it's so worthy of. Not only to God, but to each other. I can only tell you of my observations from my experience. I know they are mine. I do not think they are so different from yours. I also know that it's Time to share what we know. We are all teachers and students. We can learn from others.

The Scripture says "love thy neighbor as thyself". The Truth is we've been doing just that – we have been loving our neighbor as we love ourselves – NOT VERY WELL. We were not taught to love ourselves, to honor ourselves and yet we were taught we were made in the 'image and likeness of God'. We were told we had a soul by people who were supposed to know, and who we trusted to speak the Truth. So I say be gentle with yourself. There weren't many role models out there who understood Love, who demonstrated that understanding in their lives. I can count on one hand the number of people I know who grew up in environments of unconditional Love. And the Truth is, how can we understand something we had never experienced?

I think for many of us we could no longer accept the religious beliefs we were taught as children. And so we went Godless for a while, until the time came when we could redefine God in a way that made sense to our souls. And when we redefine God, we also redefine Love. We know now that we cannot love others until we first love ourselves.

It wasn't very long ago that I came to the realization of who God is and that God loves me unconditionally. It wasn't that long ago that I could say God loves me anyway – not if I am good or not, not if I go to church or not, not even if I love God or not – GOD'S LOVE IS UNCONDITIONAL! - that means NO CONDITIONS! - JUST IS....always and forever. God loves me anyway. And God IS Love – perfect and complete.

It wasn't that long ago that I realized that the greatest pain comes from what people say and do in the name of Love. And that is our greatest confusion. Love does not hurt. By its very nature it can't hurt. Let's be very clear. Ego hurts, judgment hurts, expectation hurts. So call it what it is – just don't call it Love. Love is God and of God.

I guess I've always believed in Love – that with Love all things were possible. I see now how God would be content to let me pursue this love thing, even when I did not pursue this God thing.

I've always believed that we human beings have a great capacity to love. It's not that we can't, we just don't know how. But we keep trying, and that's a good thing! We keep looking for true love. Well, true love is unconditional love – true love is not 'I'll love you if you love me back.' True Love is 'I love you anyway', just as God loves you and me.

And that brings up other issues, and the point is just that – what's the issue? The issue must never be Love – true love is – like God IS – it's a given. When Love is a given, then the real issues become clear – the issue may be about honesty (and usually it is) or control (and usually it is) or RESPECT (and usually it IS).

What happens when Love is a given, and we give to ourselves first? We begin to shed the old, conditional belief patterns that no longer serve this new way of being. We let go of all the stuff that does not mirror who we are becoming. And Truth stands out, and our souls move toward it. Like magnets. It takes focus and practice. We spent of a lot of years buying into conditional belief patterns – we won't relearn those patterns overnight. It takes faith and hope. It takes encouragement and trust. It takes a lot of love.

Look at the Big Picture, if you will for a moment......
From that 'root cause' of separation from God, came the **false** belief that there wasn't enough Love to go around. We were taught that God's love was limited, AND limited to a few chosen people. So we held onto what love we had, and decided we best pick and choose who we would love. And the separation widened. And the pattern continued. We can read our History books to know what happened. We can know our history to see how this great separation played out – repeating over and over, even to this day – and then let it go, for it belongs to another pattern, which is no longer who we are becoming. Many of us suffer abandonment issues, because in our hearts we believed God had abandoned us – why? Because we believed we were unworthy. Be most gentle with yourselves. God could never abandon us. Didn't God promise "I am with you always." Are you not here this day?

We are all in process of becoming who we truly are. How we do that is our own unique journey. We are all in process, we are all in different places in that process, so we must also be gentle with each other. The Native Aborigines have a great way of looking at Life. They say the same thing when a person is born and when that person dies. They say "we love and support you on your journey". This is a statement free of judgment.

They trust that the soul of each human being knows where it is going, knows what it came here to experience. They live and let live. Wise people they are. They know that we are not human beings on a soul journey – we are souls on a human journey.

So in this process of becoming we find our way. It's a journey to perfect Love. We are all born into different situations, but make no mistake, we are all deserving to share this planet. We all have a right to be here.

We all bought into the various belief systems of our childhood experiences. One of the most damaging and destructive things that can occur in a family unit is 'favoritism'. It fragments a family. It causes cracks in the foundation. The siblings do not trust each other for they are all vying for the attention and approval of the parent. Take this to the bigger picture. Favoritism has plagued our history. And it has torn apart our human family. We were taught that God has favorites, that God demands that we prove we are deserving, and that justifies what some say and do "in the name of God".

We now know that God demands nothing. GOD IS. Pray for those people who would further separate this family of God. Be gentle with them. They most especially need our love. As Jesus said "forgive them for they know not what they do". Martin Luther King said "Love is the *only force* that can turn an enemy into a friend." Send them love anyway. It may not change them, but it will change you. For hatred and love cannot dwell in the same place. And we know now that we come from Love.

And so we go along.....we thought we did everything we were supposed to do to live the perfect life. We show a great face to the world, but we dread the day we are discovered...we are empty.

And one day we have the courage to ask ourselves "is this all there is?" That is our salvation day, dear ones. It may not appear so, but God has been waiting for us to ask that very question. For then the "work" can begin. And what happens next is something like "Mr. Toad's Wild Ride" - everything changes, your life is turned upside down. OR...maybe your life was upside down and a living hell – and in despair you cried "is this all there is?" Either way, it was your wake up call. In Truth, it was a life that was not serving you, and did not nearly reflect your potential, nor your true self. But we hang onto it – until we don't. It feels uncomfortable at first, for we are breaking the chains that bind us to an old way of being, a conditioned and conditional belief pattern that has been in place for ages. Until we understand fully that God is always urging us to express at a higher level. And we trust that the new life is greater than the old. And we begin to let go of those old patterns that play over and over in our minds; we begin to grow our faith and trust that we are never alone or unaided on this journey of ours, and we begin to do what we came here to do - to remember that Love is what we are here for. It's uncomfortable.........until it's not.

We think that Love has hurt us and so we close our hearts and say we won't love again. But Love does not hurt. And Love only flows through an open heart. So how would God open our hearts? By giving us relationships. Ah, relationships! We need to understand that we are in relationship with everyone and everything around us. Everyone else is relative to where we are. Picture each of you as the center – like the sun. And everyone else moves about you. Like your own little world – truly your own reality. It gets confusing because our individual realities overlap. My reality overlaps yours at the point when we meet. And at that moment, we are in relationship.

We are already relatives. We didn't see that at first, because we were standing in a valley. But as we trust that God brings us the perfect experiences for our growth, and we have faith in ourselves, we begin to climb up that mountain, and when we are standing 'up where we belong' then we truly SEE. And what we see is that relationships afford us the greatest opportunity to know ourselves. The Gnostics say "to know oneself is to know human nature and human destiny.... to know oneself at the deepest level is to also know God."

All relationships are a transformative experience. They are designed to change us – that's the reason we're in them. All relationships have a spiritual connection. Because all relationships are ultimately about this thing called LOVE which is GOD. When we understand that we are in relationship with another human being or something the moment our lives intersect - then at almost every moment of our lives we have an opportunity to learn about or remember this thing called Love.

To those who say their hearts have been broken, I say this: thank that person or experience that came into your life – that ripped open your heart to show you how deeply you can love. Let relationship show you its true purpose. Honor it. Honor yourself in it. It is truly a holy alliance, for its purpose is Love. Above all else, be loving and gentle with yourself. The Truth is you cannot fail. The outcome is assured. You can take as long as you wish. And you will, until you don't. The pain we suffer is the resistance to this new Life that is greater than the old. The new life will not be problem-free – but you will be free.

When we get through all the stuff that no longer serves who we are we realize this:
we are really vessels for God. We are meant to be filled. With love. Perfect Love, true Love, unconditional Love. So let that vessel fill, with God's Love for you and with love of yourself. And when it

reaches the top and spills over – LET IT FLOW! And you will realize that you are being all that God intended for you to be. And in that moment your soul will rejoice, and sing and dance. You will know joy and peace. For you will be standing in the Light. And you will no longer go looking for the answers, you will know the answers are inside you – Love IS the answer.

And from that place of being, we will begin to build new patterns, based on a true foundation of unconditional love in which all God's family shares. And one day we wake up and realize that we are in the middle of this new life we created – we have changed our own little realities. And we have also changed the world. We can't see that yet. But God can see it, and that is all we need to know. We will use our given talents to express at our highest selves – our Godselves. We will create a world defined by passion, beauty, joy, peace and harmony.

There is a line from a song in Les Miserables. It says "to love another person is to see the face of God". When I look at you, I see God looking back at me. My cup runneth over. To each of you I say: I love and support you on your journey. I truly thank you for your presence in my life. It is a gift. God IS good – all the time!

4/20/1999
LD

EVERYTHING HAPPENS
FOR OUR GOOD

I remember saying during times of stress, uncertainty, doubt, frustration, etc.: *"this is for my good – I just don't know why yet"*. I did not fully comprehend that statement for years. And yet, I knew intuitively that I was onto something BIG.

Life operates in 'paradox': "do the opposite to find Truth", and this was one of those paradoxes that I would come to truly understand and welcome.

Out of everything that happens to us, there is a blessing. It's a little like walking through fire, and some life coaches do call it the 'ring of fire'. We don't see the blessing, or more importantly, *feel* the blessing, because it's happening *inside* us. Our challenges are bringing up conditioned beliefs that no longer serve us but they may lie buried deep in our subconscious, and it's our subconscious belief systems that are running our lives. It becomes how we see the world in which we live – it is our own perception that creates our experiences.

It is also said that "choice is a function of awareness". Some people don't even believe they have a choice over their lives. I don't think Life is about acquiring the most things to make ourselves comfortable. Yes, comfort, safety, families we love and love us, work we love is important. More important is the evolution of our soul and our connection with our Creator, a Source greater than ourselves. That is the true journey we are on.....the journey back to our Source.

Our awakenings are the 'aha' moments of great clarity, intuition and eventually trust in that Source.

If we knew that, wouldn't we also know that everything *does* happen for our good, because that Source is always urging us to grow and be more.

What I have realized that though everything happens for our good, not everything *feels* good. Why? Because we are being pruned. The LOVE we choose is burning the old beliefs, and we feel like we are dying. But we are not. We are following the same laws of Nature. We are laying the fields fallow for planting new seeds and birthing new beliefs. And new Life!

Some people coach "lean into the pain". The Runes say "sit with the pain". In other words, don't run from the pain or avoid your feelings – lean into them to get at those root notions that have kept you prisoners of your own beliefs. It takes courage and patience; the outcome is assured – new life! Peace, clarity, and most importantly Trust. It only takes willingness…..you are going that way anyway! So why resist?

\\\\\\

In 2000, after losing a job, I had to sell my home.

For the next 2 ½ years I experienced what I have come to call "a walk in Faith". From the outside it looked as if I had lost my mind. I recall one friend saying I had a 'breakdown' when in fact, I had a 'breakthrough'. All illusion fell away and I had made a 'flip' – to my inner being. Well, to some that would seem like I was crazy. What I absolutely *knew* was that how I thought about the experience would create my future: would I be on the street, homeless? Or would I put complete faith and trust in the Invisible realm to support and guide me through this passage. Yes, the experience did push every button of ego and fear I possessed. It did make me claim that "this was happening for my good – I just didn't know why yet". It was almost unbearable to be separated from my children, but I knew they would be cared for by their father. I told them this was all temporary and that I would be OK. And I was!

If I never properly thanked all those earth angels that came to my rescue let me say I am so grateful to you and for you at that time in my life.

In truth, the whole Universe conspires to assist and support us to wake up. In hindsight, we see this and know this......when it's happening we just have to trust, breathe and keep moving. One gets very focused and single-minded – intuition kicks into high gear and we get still and listen – and let the Mind of God lead us. Not easy. The miracle is that I'm here to write about it!

What I did during that time was to be a care-taker of sorts. It was women that took me in, and women who needed care-taking. A wise 'angel' remarked how many people I helped because I didn't have a "real" job.

When the going gets tough, I walk. When I don't know what to do, I walk. Julia Cameron teaches: "your soul talks to you through your soles". That drove people crazy.
You see, the answers came......while I walked!
And only the next step, but that's all I needed.

In fact, my whole experience made others most uncomfortable. Only I knew what was happening, because it was happening *inside* me. Inside me – my inner being was changing so rapidly that nothing would 'stick' in the outer realm. Even writing this will cause some to think I've completely lost my mind. Well, partly true – I did come to be 'out of my mind' and in the realm of Reality. That's Reality with a capital R – quite different.

The experience grew my faith and trust. As usual, my wise children would send me cards that said "keep the faith"….a reminder that faith was all I had. As Marianne Williamson teaches "when you're down on your knees, stay there".

My life looked pretty weird. Very few understood.
Even I had my doubts. "This Day" served me well.

As Life would have it, after a time I found myself in Santa Barbara, living by the ocean. When I knew I was going there I laughed. "Oh I see" I said. "I'm going to the ocean to rest and heal." Every day I could go the ocean and sit on the bluffs and take in the view of that big, wide ocean and feel how I was a part of it all. I felt like I had been blown to bits and now was coming back together – whole, in the knowing of Who's I was. The ocean was in front of me and the hills were behind me and they were alive with sound and music to my ears and my soul. Indeed, the earth sings a melody and cradles us – our Mother Earth.

While living in Santa Barbara, I asked a resident teacher I met how people survived living in this expensive place. She told me many lived on trust funds. That resonated with me, because I too live on a trust fund – I trust in God with all my heart!
That was the blessing that came from my experience.

And the other blessing was the 'peace that surpasses understanding' that resonates in my being. A paradox!

Here's what I have to say about that experience:

I am not the first mother to be separated from her children. I would like to be the last. Though we are bound in Spirit, let us honor that in the flesh.

In our thoughts – let us see the feminine in all of Life.

In our words – let us honor the feminine as we honor the masculine.

In our work – let us make motherhood holy work. Let fatherhood be supportive of motherhood.

I see a world where all life is sacred. All beings are equal – no one more important than another.

I see a world that lives in peace: in Harmony with God, the earth and each other.

With God, all things are possible.

Amen!

When we do the demanding work of looking at our life experiences in new light, we see that all of Life is for us – that everything happens the way it should.

Saying that leads us to review our lives and see from a different perspective and perception – the good in all experiences, simply because God is in all experiences. God is in all of life – infusing it with Love as our very life Itself. What I can confirm is that we live in a friendly Universe that is always supporting our growth, our good. Yes, the "being there experience" is the best teacher!

Suffering produces Endurance.

Endurance produces Character.

Character produces Faith.

And Faith, in the end, will not disappoint.

Harriet Tubman
The Woman Called Moses

My Faith was tested. I believe the point of Faith *IS* to be tested. That's how we grow our Faith. The experiences of our lives also help us to grow closer to our Source. To learn that we are not alone – ever!

Here's another paradox: as we go further into our core, we expand our being beyond our own visible selves. We connect to that invisible web that supports us, inspires us...the very Source of our being.

I often think of how wise the fairy tales are. We learned about them as children, and revisit them when we have our own children. They hold more Truth than we acknowledge. Just as in dreams, we can become every character in the story and see how those principles play out in our lives.

It helps, as women, to know we can rescue ourselves and not wait for the prince in shining armor. (because we are the princess in shining armor!)

It furthers our resolve to let love and kindness break down the barriers we see as beast.

It reminds us that we are "great, cosmic power in itty, bitty living spaces" – our genies.(genius)

And while on the topic of fairy tales, I am reminded that in many of them, the mother dies or is not there at all. If she were, none of the story would unfold the way it does. Her part is sorely missing.

We do need to reclaim Mothers' roles in our world. She is sorely missing. Mother's work is sacred work.
But she cannot do it alone.

I wonder what the world would look like if we honored and supported this sacred work. If we honored and supported all children everywhere. If we made their safety and growth our collective work. I wonder what the earth would look like if we realized that it too is our Mother, and we walk on holy ground everywhere we go.

We would protect and preserve, not conquer and destroy.
We would create "on earth as it is in heaven".
We would know Peace.
We would see through the eyes of our children.

***

There are times in our lives when we are ready to
advance. Just like in school – only this is the School
of Life! I have Rev. Jenenne Macklin and the Living
in the Light Ministry to thank for this next piece.
And for the love and support I truly felt while there.
It was Rev. Jenenne who truly helped me find my voice,
and gave me room to practice. She asked me to
speak on the eve of the new century. I still believe
and affirm what follows:

Celebration of Light Service: Dec. 31, 1999
Living in the Light Ministry

Please pray with me:
I dream a world of Light. Our brilliant selves shining through this
costume, our humanness. We are just dusting over a soul. A soul
that is light – free and flowing - dancing. We are here. We know
Dear God, that You are here with us. All is well. Help us to know
Your will for us. Amen

We have entered the Age of Aquarius, the Age of Enlightenment.
This is the Age of spiritual enlightenment, when the soul will know
it is home and that home is Here and Now – when Heaven touches
down to meet Earth in that place called You. We are not unaided
in this endeavor. God is working overtime, and the whole Universe
supports this great shift in consciousness. We have conquered outer
space but the shift that is occurring is concerned with inner space.
For just as we gaze at the heavens and take in the wonder and
vastness of the Universe *out* there, there is just as vast and wondrous
a Universe *in* here, the Light within us. Not just in some of us. In
all of us. For we all come from the same Source. We are all divine
expressions of God. And we are on our way home. We have made

a journey round the world to find ourselves back where we started. And we realize that the starting point is the self.

The Gnostics were a sect of Christianity, whose teachings were all but destroyed around 400 A.D. The word Gnosis comes from the Greek and means "to know". The Gnostics said "know thyself...to know thyself is to know all of human nature, and to know thyself at the deepest level is to know God". This knowing comes from within. It is profound wisdom that comes in moments of silence, in stillness, when the soul is at rest.

I have always loved looking at the stars at night. They are not so visible where I live, but we also have a place on the Colorado River. It's out in the desert, where there are no city lights to obstruct the view. And what a view it is! There must be millions of stars, and I often wonder - if we were out there on one of those stars looking back at earth, would we also see stars? I believe the answer is yes – we would. The Universe mirrors to us what we are – brilliant lights. It reminds me of a poem by Shel Silverstein I read to my boys:

"somebody has to polish the stars, they're looking a little bit dull.."

We are doing just that. And we do it by letting go of the old beliefs, the old patterns that no longer serve us.
We do it when we choose to have new thoughts about our beings, our relationship to God and to each other.
I wish to talk about a particular star – Albert Einstein.
Albert Einstein has been chosen Person of the Century by Time Magazine. Certainly we can agree that he had one of the greatest minds of our time, even if we don't quite grasp E=mc2. One writer made it clear for me – what Einstein theorized was that Energy and Matter were different faces for the same thing.

What may not be so well known was that he was a man of great conviction and a deep belief in God and God's goodness. He said that he approached his work like a child imagining the mind of God. He simply opened up to infinite possibilities, with child-like wonder. He had a gentle manner and a great reverence for Life. People said he was absentminded and often couldn't remember where he lived. But I think that was because he LIVED everywhere he went. He was alive to the beauty and symmetry that exists in the Universe. He said "Imagination is greater than knowledge." That in taking imaginative leaps, a scientist could catch a glimpse of the Universe as it really is, and not as it merely appears to be. He knew that it was in this realm of imagination that God was saying: congratulations, you are out of your mind, and moving closer to the mysteries of the Universe.

We have prized our minds in leading us forward in this materialistic, technological world. But we have left out a most important element – our hearts.

It is time to think with our hearts. It is time to move, not forward, but inward. It is time for us to take an imaginative leap of faith and begin to imagine how God would create a world where all human beings can live in peace and abundance. Where no one goes hopeless, hungry, homeless, and NO ONE fears for their life for any reason! Don't you wonder how God would do that! Those answers are within us - waiting for us to tap into them. We must begin to ask different questions, or ask the same questions from a different place.

There is no pleasing the ego-mind that wants proof. We must ask from a heart that is open and trusting – like a child's. When the Ego-mind asks "'God, show me your face.''– nothing appears. When the heart asks "God, show me your face" – a small voice within you says "dear one, you have only to look in the mirror, or turn your head and look at your neighbor." Jesus said "You have eyes but cannot see." That is because the most important things can only be seen with the heart.

We agree that miracles are God's love expressing in the world. And miracles have everything to do with timing........ God shows up just in the nick of time. Einstein said this:
There are two ways to live your life:
One is as though nothing is a miracle.
The other is as though everything is a miracle.

Believe in miracles? Are you out of your mind? God is right on time and it's TIME. It's time for this new world to manifest.
And what better time than this night, at the dawn of a new century, to affirm this to the Universe and let it be.

My son Eddie asked me once "Mama, do you think we are dreaming, and when we die we wake up?" Yes, my little wise one, I do think it's a lot like that. We ARE dreaming, but we don't have to physically die to wake up. We die each time we let go of old patterns, old beliefs, things we once bought into but now know are not Truth. We change. Actually, we become a little less tarnished. In that death is a rebirth – a transformation - an awakening to our true purpose here: To manifest the glory of God within us. Not in some of us – in all of us. And to return this world to love.

"Somebody has to polish the stars, they're looking a little bit dull.…..."

I've been coming to Living in the Light for a year now. And I know that's what Rev. Macklin and this Ministry are doing every Sunday.......polishing stars.
A great leader doesn't create followers. A great leader creates other leaders. Thank you, Rev. Macklin. Follow your star, your light. It will lead you to the center of your being, where there are NO impossible dreams. You are the dreamer. You are the dreamed. I dream a world of Light, our brilliant selves shining...........

"So please get your rags
And your polishing jars,
Somebody has to go polish the stars."

And just in case the ego mind was asking………... Yes, there is a God.
In front of me, behind me, within me. Loving me. And that IS a miracle. Thank you all for your presence in my life. We convince with our presence, and as we shine our light we give others permission to shine theirs. There is a unique contribution each of us makes to this holy endeavor. Go within and find that treasure. God is there waiting for you, to show you the way. It is all within you. And so it is. And so we are…….shining lights………brilliant stars. I love you back.
God bless us everyone. Thank you, God.

("Somebody has to polish the stars" by Shel Silverstein)

NOW

I wrote this book over 15 years ago. Interestingly, it stands the test of Time. Because Truth is timeless, and perhaps what I have written here will resonate with others and together we will make the changes necessary for this world of ours to know Peace.

Over the past few years, some of that "polishing" has to do with women. Namely women supporting women instead of competing with them.

I have been blessed to still have contact with childhood girlfriends and over the years, as we have all mellowed, I see how we are just happy to be alive and still in touch. We don't compare our lives and I suspect we each would keep our own.

And it's given me pause to think how we are taught to compete so early on. Girls competing with girls for the favors of men.

What I know now is that the World reflects the favoritism that places men over women. How many cultures and religions favor men! It is no wonder that women do not trust each other – we are taught early on to compete – with each other.

What I know now is that the World is quite unbalanced because of this favoritism toward men.

In A Mother's Prayer I write:

> To be honored as a bridge
> for peace and harmony
> All over the world

Motherhood is sacred work – it needs all hands to bring forth a different future.

As a mother I know that I did not raise boys to go off to war – not when there is another way to resolve differences.

And if women's voices were heard I believe there would be no more war.

If women's voices were heard there would be cooperation, not competition. Womanhood is inclusive by nature.

If women's voices were heard we would get the support to raise children in safe places – all our children.

If women' voices were heard.....
I know that I stand with women around the world –
in love and support – and unity – to be heard.

I also know that over the past twenty years I have come to honor the sacred work that women contribute to our world. I have been privileged to have had many mothers in my life and I wish to continue that legacy by mentoring young women.

Perhaps my experience and my writings will be a source for new patterns.

Something that has become very 'clear' to me in the past few years is how paradigms are shifting, and on a broader scale we are changing from 'dominator' pattern to 'partnership' pattern.

In our thinking we are changing from an 'either/or' pattern to an 'and' pattern. We are shifting from win/lose patterns to win/win patterns.

Another definition for paradigm is declension of a verb. As in:

I am	We are
You are	You are
He/she is	They are

Here's the new paradigm (pattern) emerging:

I am AND You are AND He/She is AND
We are AND You are AND They are

ALL LIFE IS SACRED. Men AND Women
(who were once boys and girls)

It's a Mindshift to be sure, but it is happening. The resistance is the 'status-quo' or the old order, the old pattern. That 'old order' has come into our conscious mind – to make clear the patterns that have been driving us and running automatically – until we say STOP – and ask the question: Is this the world we want for our children?

I believe it is not...........

DRUMMERS

The ancient drummers call to me.
I feel their drumbeat through Eternity.
Through the tunnel of yesterday and tomorrow,
    I call to them and they to me.
To meet me here on the plain of reckoning, David and Goliath – my greatest battle,
the test I meet, bravely and courageously with my self.
Against the great mountain of what is – is no more......
For I turn in the face of all opposition
    I shall not fail
    I shall not be undone, only transformed
    I shall put down my sword and walk away,
    the battle won.

I march to a different drummer, whose beat was even before you and I were.
Who claimed me as Its own, wholly pleasing,
    and breathed life into my loins.

Put away from you any thought that makes a mockery of this Holy Thought: the
Divine experiences Itself in ALL that lives. All Life is Sacred.

As Mother I claim sacred this earth from which we rise, and shall return.
You shall honor my gifts and as long as you walk upon me, gratitude shall be your
prayer, thankfulness shall be your song.
A full heart can only praise its Maker.

As Father I claim sacred this Mother and the fruits of her womb - to protect, support,
encourage, empower.

I no longer carry the banner into battle, but am the rudder to my Lady's lead.
Her gentle honor the medal I wear, her love my only possession, her beauty my
reward.

That at the end of the day she cast her moon shadow upon my sun, and give rest to
my soul.
And a circle we shall make, to sleep safe in the arms of peace, and the goodness of
the life we share.

6-4-2000 LD

Being a student and facilitator of The Artist's Way since 1994 gave me the clarity and courage to pursue the career I longed for as a child and even went to school for as a young adult, but didn't actually work at until my early 50's.

The Artist's Way is a process to unblocking creativity. It holds that our creativity comes from God and using it is our gift back to God. My first love was always the Home. Even as a child I would cut out pictures from magazines and put them in a book. I was always wanting to 'set the table' for my Mom and make it pretty. My sister once remarked that I was going to have a beautiful home when I grew up. And eventually I did!

Textiles were my 'true love' and I learned to sew clothing and eventually I sewed for the homes I lived in. I was honing my skills, and poured over magazines to discover my style.

I was in sales most of my life. Not because I was good at it, but because I needed to get good at it. The jobs I held gave me the greatest opportunity to learn about people and more importantly, myself.

I learned from one wise teacher: "relationships sell product", and I heeded that wisdom and took it to heart. I learned to trust a win/win relationship with the people I worked with and for. I learned to be open and honest and be myself. I recall one customer saying that I could "sell snowshoes in the desert". A great compliment to a shy girl!
Although I decorated all the homes I lived in and would also consult with family members, I didn't actually work at interior design until my early 50's.

I have worked with some wonderful people who have become dear friends. I have had the privilege of being invited into homes to help the owners create a nurturing space to live. And in the process I have honed my eye and edited my style and I surmise that process will continue.

Life is a lot like that.

When I heard Einstein's quote: "Imagination is more important than knowledge" I knew that was Truth. And it validated all my yearnings as a child, and I vowed that I would not stifle my own children's creativity.

What I have found is that creativity itself doesn't cost a thing! But it can be stifled when we put a "budget" on it. We limit it when we attach a dollar amount to it. In my experience, not having lots of money for decorating made me be more innovative, and perhaps you might say *more* creative, but it did put a damper on my dreaming and visioning what might be possible for me and my life.

I believe that our dreams were put in our hearts by our Creator. We ARE dreaming – all the time. LOVING our dreams is what will eventually manifest them in the world we see. Love IS the answer.

What I have found is that I love to create! I love the whole process – from conception to seeing the finished product. We creators know when we are "in the zone" and ideas are flying and so is time.
We become focused and tune out any distractions.
I love to create nurturing spaces. That's how I see my work.

Over the years my son Ed, who did grow up to be a fabulous artist, would design business cards for me. For the most recent card we collaborated on, Ed again said "keep it simple". My business card simply says

'Create Home'

I remember looking at that line and felt intuitively that it was telling me something.............

Create HOME.......Harmony On Mother Earth
Home is where we start from and not everyone has been afforded the great advantage of living in safe, nurturing spaces.

"......where no one goes homeless, or hungry, and no one fears for their life for any reason"

Focusing on the needs of ALL our children will bring about the Harmony and the Peace we all truly desire.

For our children, and our children's children.

How do we do that? We begin by visualizing it!
And we don't wait for permission – we just do it!

It can happen!

With God, all things are possible!

NOTE: As I send this to the publishers we have just witnessed the Women's March in this country.
Women supporting women, not competing with women. Because that's who we really are.

YES! God is right on time!

BRIDGE OF PEACE

Imagine there's a space between you and me
We're standing face to face across Eternity.
One heartbeat to another, arms open to embrace –
This most sacred space – this Bridge of Peace.

Imagine there's a time that's neither young nor old.
We're standing in this moment complete, forever whole. All ages
and all kinds, arms open to embrace –
This most sacred time on this timeless Bridge of Peace.

You can travel round the world, you can stand real still. You can
climb the highest mountain and never win until you see me through
your heart and mine, knowing we're Divine. And reach across all
space and time upon this Bridge of Peace.

Stand forever by my side, let our voices change the tide. Then we'll
sing "let freedom ring" In Love we will abide.
Heart to heart, face to face, my friend this is the place.
We're standing in amazing grace upon this Bridge of Peace.

There's no better time or place, we know that Love's the way, and
we can find it every day upon a Bridge of Peace.

LD

"Blessed are the peacemakers for they shall be called

Children of God"

THE BEATITUDES

Amen

ACKNOWLEDGMENTS

First and foremost, I wish to acknowledge God as my Source and my life.

I thank all those who have journeyed with me...
my parents, my siblings, my childhood friends,
my family of friends now; especially those who know me and love me anyway. We're all relatives!

The Angels and the Wise Men....my humble thanks!

I thank my spiritual advisors —especially Rev. Macklin and Living in the Light Ministry and all its members.
Also, much gratitude for Unity, the Daily Word,
and Agape Spiritual Center of Truth.

In particular, I thank Julia Cameron and The Artist's Way, and the process of the Morning Pages. I have written them for more than 24 years. They have sustained me in drought and plenty. Such a gift, Julia! "I am a believing mirror."

Mostly I am thankful for the Love that abides in me - for my children and children everywhere.

You can't lose what's in your heart.
LD

References

www.AcupunctureNowFoundation.org
Matthew D. Bauer,.Ac., President

http://www.sueteele.net
Study of Multiple Intelligence

http://www.randomactsofkindness.org
for spreading kindness

www.lifelab.com
school garden resources
garden-based learning

distarce.myportfolio.com
artistry of Edward Distarce